TREKKING IN THE APENNINES

GEA – GRANDE ESCURSIONE APPENNINICA

About the Author

Gillian Price was born in England but moved to Australia when young. After a degree in anthropology and work in adult education, she set off to travel through Asia and trek the Himalayas. The culmination of her journey was Venice where, her enthusiasm for mountains fired, the next logical step was towards the Dolomites, only hours away. Starting there, Gillian is steadily exploring the mountain ranges of Italy and bringing them to life for visitors in a series of outstanding guides for Cicerone. When not out walking with her Venetian cartographer husband, Gillian works as a travel writer www.gillianprice.eu. An ardent promoter of public transport to minimise impact in alpine areas, she is an active member of the Italian Alpine Club CAI and Mountain Wilderness.

Other Cicerone guides by the author

Across the Eastern Alps – the E5
Alpine Flowers
Gran Paradiso: Alta Via 2 Trek and
    Day Walks
Italy's Sibillini National Park
Italy's Stelvio National Park
Shorter Walks in the Dolomites
The Tour of the Bernina
Through the Italian Alps – the GTA
Trekking in the Alps (contributor)
Trekking in the Dolomites

Walking in the Central Italian Alps
Walking in Corsica
Walking in the Dolomites
Walking in Sicily
Walking in Tuscany
Walking in Umbria
Walking the Italian Lakes
Walking on the Amalfi Coast
Walking and Trekking on Corfu
Walks and Treks in the Maritime
    Alps

TREKKING IN THE APENNINES

GEA – GRANDE ESCURSIONE APPENNINICA

by Gillian Price

2 POLICE SQUARE, MILNTHORPE, CUMBRIA LA7 7PY
www.cicerone.co.uk

© Gillian Price 2015
Second edition 2015
ISBN: 978 1 85284 766 1
First edition 2005
ISBN: 978 1 85284 416 5
Printed by KHL Printing, Singapore
A catalogue record for this book is available from the British Library.
All photographs are by the author unless otherwise stated.
Maps by Nicola Regine.

Acknowledgements

Heaps of thanks to Anna, Colleen, Daniele, Laura, Clive and Lucy for their immensely enjoyable company on the trail, Marty for a route check, the woodcutters and hunters who pointed us in the right direction the first time, CAI branches for practical information, the rifugi cooks for their delectable bilberry tarts and Giorgio Baruffini of Parma for his help with those place name explanations that so intrigue me.

Thanks to my publisher Jonathan, who said 'yes' once again, the great team at Cicerone who put the book together, the many readers who kindly sent in updates for the first edition and, last but nowhere least, to Nicola for the maps.

Updates to this Guide

While every effort is made by our authors to ensure the accuracy of guidebooks as they go to print, changes can occur during the lifetime of an edition. Any updates that we know of for this guide will be on the Cicerone website (www.cicerone.co.uk/766/updates), so please check before planning your trip. We also advise that you check information about such things as transport, accommodation and shops locally. Even rights of way can be altered over time. We are always grateful for information about any discrepancies between a guidebook and the facts on the ground, sent by email to info@cicerone.co.uk or by post to Cicerone, 2 Police Square, Milnthorpe LA7 7PY, United Kingdom.

Front cover: Between Monte Marmagna and Monte Braiola (Stage 22).

CONTENTS

Map key

═══════════	sealed road	⌂	accommodation
▪▪▪▪▪▪▪□▪▪▪▪▪▪▪	railway + station	⌂	bivouac hut
▬▬▬▬▬▬▬	walk route	🛒	groceries
▪▪▪▪▪▪▪▪▪▪▪▪	walk variant	🚌	bus
Ⓢ	start point	🚂	train
Ⓕ	finish point	🚠	cable car
†	church, shrine, chapel	▲	mountain peak

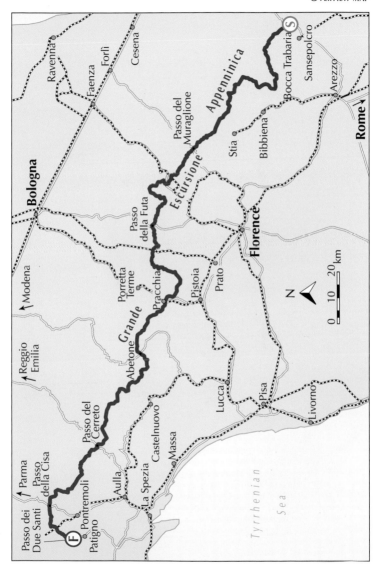

On the way up to Colle Bruciata (Stage 17)

PREFACE TO THE SECOND EDITION

Between Colla di Casaglia and Badia Moscheta (Stage 7)

After 10 years away from the Apennine mountains, it was with great pleasure – and relief – that I discovered very little has changed on this memorable trek. Long rambles in solitude are still the flavour of the day, while a steady trickle of pilgrims on the Franciscan trails are now found in the trek's southern parts. The forests are still vast and magical, the village inhabitants as friendly as ever and the meals thankfully mouth-wateringly delicious. The few notable differences – changes for the better – are the hugely improved waymarking and the places where the GEA has been rerouted to take in more superbly scenic ridges and summits.

Gillian Price, 2015

En route to Poggio Scali (Stage 5)

INTRODUCTION

Heading towards Libro Aperto (Stage 15)

Your peaks are beautiful, ye
Apennines!
In the soft light of these serenest
skies;
From the broad highland region,
black with pines,
Fair as the hills of Paradise they rise.
*To the Apennines, William Cullen
Bryant, 1835*

The mountainous Apennines, without
a doubt, are Italy's best-kept secret.
Forming the rugged spine of the slender Italian peninsula, they seem to
provide support as it ventures out
into the Mediterranean. For walkers
this glorious elongated range provides
thousands of kilometres of marked

walking trails over stunning panoramic
ridges and stupendous forested valleys,
touching on quiet rural communities
little affected by mass tourism. Dotted
throughout are historic sanctuaries,
hospitable mountain inns, national
parks and nature reserves home to
wildlife and marvellous wildflowers,
incredible roads and passes that tes-
tify to feats of engineering, and stark
memorials to the terrible events of
World War II.

THE APENNINES

The Apennine chain runs along the
entire length of Italy and clocks up
some 1400km from the link with the

Alps close to the French border, all the way south to the Straits of Messina, even extending over to Sicily. The highest peak is the 2912m Corno Grande in Italy's southern Abruzzo region. As a formidable barrier that splits the country in two lengthways, the range has witnessed centuries of wars and skirmishes, alternating with the passage of traders, pilgrims and daring bandits.

The rock is, by and large, sedimentary in nature – sandstone, shale and some limestone – deposited in an ancient sea during the Mesozoic era (245–66 million years ago). The mountains were formed immediately after their neighbours, the Alps, when – some 66 million years ago, and climaxing around two million years BCE – remnants of the African plate were forced together and squeezed upwards, little by little.

Both volcanic and seismic activity shaped the Apennines, though ancient ice masses also played a part. Tell-tale clues are sheltered cirques like giant armchairs, once filled by ice from a glacier tongue and nowadays more often than not home to a lake or tarn. The present aspect of the Apennines – steep, rough western flanks overlooking the Tyrrhenian Sea, in contrast to the relatively gentler slopes on the eastern Adriatic side – is due mainly to recent erosion by water.

Evidence has been unearthed of man's presence since prehistoric times, some 7000 years ago. The northern Apennines were then the stronghold of the ancient Liguri or Ligurian people (as the colonising Romans found out to their detriment over the 150 years it took to get the fierce tribes to accept domination). We are probably indebted to them for the very name Apennines: the root 'penn' (for an isolated peak) is found throughout Italy. In another version Pennine was a divinity believed to reside on the inhospitable summits, while a further interpretation attributes the name to King Api, last of the Italic gods.

Over time well-trodden paths conveyed waves of passers-by, such as devotees on the Via Francigena which led from Canterbury to Rome. For the great medieval poet Dante Alighieri, the Apennines were a source of inspiration for 'The Divine Comedy'; the same holds true for Petrarch and Boccaccio. German writer Johann Wolfgang von Goethe, revelling in sun-blessed Italy, was heading south towards Rome in October 1786, and wrote: 'I find the Apennines a remarkable part of the world. Upon the great plain of the Po basin there follows a mountain range that rises from the depths, between two seas, to end the continent on the south…it is a curious web of mountain ridges facing each other.'

From their base near the Tyrrhenian coast, both Mary and Percy Bysshe Shelley were inspired by the Apennines, which made appearances in their respective works *Valperga* and 'The Witch of Atlas'.

Lovely Lago Scaffaiolo (Stage 14)

The 'romantic' wild woods and mountainous ridges were long the realm of smugglers, woodcutters and charcoal burners. The latter were renowned as a wild mob who moved from camp to camp erecting huge compact mounds of cut branches that underwent slow round-the-clock combustion. Their circular cleared work platforms are still visible. Plaques recording the passage of indefatigable Giuseppe Garibaldi are not unusual. Instigator of the unification of northern Italy with Sicily and the south in 1861 under the Kingdom of the House of Savoy, he crossed the Apennines on one of his campaigns, his ranks swelled by Robin Hood-style bandits in revolt in the Romagna region against harsh taxes and the Austrian occupation.

The central and northern Apennines were subjected to widespread devastation in the latter years of World War II. Once fascist Italy had recapitulated and signed a peace agreement with the Allies in 1943, the Germans turned into occupying forces and dug themselves in to prepare for the inevitable advance which thankfully led to the liberation of the whole country in 1945. Massive defences were constructed in 1944 – the so-called Gothic Line – that stretched coast-to-coast across the peninsula, entailing drastically clearing ridges to enable control of strategic passes along with key communication routes. Although a sea of green has now all but obliterated signs of battle, there are poignant reminders in the shape of war cemeteries and memorials to the Italian partisans, former soldiers who sprang into action after the armistice, working closely in liaison with Allied servicemen parachuted in behind the lines.

THE GEA TREK

The trek described in this guide is a memorable long-distance journey on foot snaking its way through the central and northern section of the Apennines. The Grande Escursione Appenninica or GEA (pronounced 'jayah' in Italian) spends a total of 23 wonderful days covering a little over 400km (402.6km to be precise), approximately a third of the total length of the Apennine chain; it moves across altitudes ranging between 400 and 2054m above sea level. Accommodation en route is in comfortable guesthouses and alpine-style refuges.

Starting in eastern Tuscany on the border with Umbria and the Marche, the trek progresses northwest to make a number of forays into Emilia-Romagna – with marked changes in accents and cuisine – before heading inland parallel to the Tyrrhenian coast on its way north to the edge of Liguria.

The route was conceived in the 1980s by Florentine walking enthusiasts Alfonso Bietolini and Gianfranco Bracci, though many improvements have since been implemented. The walking is straightforward, on paths, forestry tracks and lanes with constant waymarking, making the GEA suitable for a broad range of walkers. In the northern part the odd brief tract negotiates exposed crest, mostly avoidable. The terrain ranges from rocky slopes and open windswept crests,

Marvellous views over the Garfagnana to the Alpi Apuane (Stage 17)

thick carpets of flowered meadows through to woods, where layers of leaf litter provide a soft cushion for tired feet and the play of sunlight serves as distraction from fatigue. Almost every day road passes and villages served by local transport are touched on, enabling walkers to slot in or bail out at will, to fit in with personal holiday requirements.

The initial southernmost sections of the GEA traverse the 364 sq km Parco Nazionale delle Foreste Casentinesi, which boasts magnificent spreads of ancient chestnut, fir and beech wood lovingly nurtured over the centuries by monks. Here at times the route coincides with pathways taken by Saint Francis as he tramped the hills setting up isolated retreats and spreading his message of simplicity. Nowadays groups of pilgrims follow in his footsteps on their way to Assisi. The second, more elevated part of the trek where the Apennines overlook the intensively cultivated Po plain, comes under the auspices of the fledgling 240 sq km Parco Nazionale dell'Appennino Tosco-Emiliano, dotted with sparkling lakes, formed in ancient times by long-gone glaciers.

HIGHLIGHTS AND SHORTER WALKS

The GEA is well suited for biting off sizeable chunks as single or multiple-day walks thanks to the excellent network of public transport that serves the Apennine villages and passes. To facilitate walkers who don't have 23 days available for the entire trek, a selection of shorter sections encompassing highlights is outlined here. Each begins and ends at a location served directly by public transport (or within reasonable distance). In the absence of a bus, you can always ask at a café or hotel for a local taxi.

- **1 day** Badia Prataglia–Camaldoli (Stage 5). Straightforward paths climb through divine woods to a broad ridge, whence a plunge to a landmark historic sanctuary and monastery.
- **1 day** Passo del Giogo–Passo della Futa (Stage 10). A roller-coaster day that concludes at a poignant World War II German war cemetery.
- **1–2 days** Montepiano–Rifugio Pacini–Cantagallo (Stages 12 and 13). Studded with shrines this wander through the vast sea of rolling green hills is a delight in springtime.
- **2 days** Badia Prataglia–Rifugio Città di Forlì–Passo del Muraglione (Stages 5 and 6). A rewarding mini-trek through the Casentino National Park, taking in forests, high peaks and scenic crests, not to mention some good hospitality.
- **2 days** Pracchia–Lago Scaffaiolo–Abetone (Stages 14 and 15). Exhilarating if tiring stretch that negotiates both beautiful woodland where deer abound and

breathtaking open ridges, touching on two key peaks.

- **2 days** Boscolungo (Abetone)–Lago Santo Modenese–San Pellegrino in Alpe (Stages 16 and 17). Some marvellous panoramic ridge walking, a justifiably popular lake resort and a historic sanctuary as the final destination.

- **2 days** Prato Spilla–Lago Santo Parmense–Passo della Cisa (Stages 21 and 22). Plenty of open ridge with massive sweeping views,

PROMINENT PEAKS IN THE NORTHERN APPENINES

The following panoramic peaks are all included in the trek or reachable via a brief detour:

- 1520m Poggio Scali (Stage 5)
- 1657m Monte Falco (Stage 6)
- 1945m Corno alle Scale (Stage 14)
- 1936m Libro Aperto (Stage 15)
- 1935m Alpe Tre Potenze (Stage 16)
- 1964m Monte Rondinaio (Stage 16)
- 1780m Cime del Romecchio (Stage 17)

- 1708m Cima La Nuda (Stage 18)
- 2054m Monte Prado (Stage 18)
- 1895m Monte La Nuda (Stage 19)
- 1859m Monte Sillara (Stage 21)
- 1851m Monte Marmagna (Stage 22)
- 1830m Monte Orsaro (Stage 22)

Monte Prado, the highest peak in Tuscany

while myriad attractive lakes nestling in cirques provide good excuses for a detour. It takes in one of the best sections of the entire trek.

- **3 days** Passo delle Radici–Passo Pradarena–Passo del Cerreto (Stages 18 and 19). Another unbeatable 'top' section that boasts brilliant views, the highest peak in Tuscany and the GEA, and premium bilberry 'orchards'.

WILDLIFE

Roe deer and timid fallow deer are numerous all along the Apennine chain and are easy to spot grazing on the edge of woods in the early morning and late afternoon. Majestic red deer are more rarely seen, mostly in the heavily forested Parco Nazionale delle Foreste Casentinesi. Originally introduced from northern Europe in the 1800s in the interests of the game reserve belonging to the Grand-Duke of Tuscany Leopold II, their numbers were boosted in the 1950s and the population, now estimated at around two thousand, is the largest in the whole of the Apennines.

A more recent arrival is the marmot, which hails from the Alps. Modest colonies can be observed in the northern Apennines at elevations between 1000 and 2000m. A burrowing rodent resembling a beaver or ground hog, its habitat is stony pasture slopes. The trick in spotting these cuddly comical creatures is to listen out for the piercing shriek of alarm from the sentry on the lookout for eagles, their sole enemy. Marmots spend the summer feasting on flowers and grass with the aim of doubling their body weight in preparation for hibernation

Inquisitive goats and horses check out walkers on the GEA

around October; they re-emerge in springtime.

Then there is the wild boar, a great nuisance in view of the inordinate damage it wreaks, rooting around in cultivated fields and woodland. Scratchings, hoofprints and ripped-up undergrowth along with curious mudslides are commonly encountered signs of its presence, though the closest most walkers will get to one is stewed on a restaurant plate at dinnertime as, despite their reputation for fierceness, they are notoriously reticent. The thriving modern-day population is the offspring of prolific Eastern European species introduced to supplement the native population for the purposes of hunting, a collective sport practised with unflagging enthusiasm since Roman times. In adherence to a strict calendar – usually in the November–January period – vociferous armed groups tramp hillsides and woods with yapping dogs sniffing out the elusive creatures.

In woodland the eccentric crested porcupine is not uncommon, but incredibly timid (not to mention nocturnal). Its calling cards are striking black-and-cream quills found on many a pathway, often denoting a struggle with an optimistic predator. The ancient Romans, ever the epicures, brought it over from Africa for its tasty flesh, a great delicacy at banquets (along with dormouse).

Anti-social badgers, on the other hand, leave grey tubes of excrement, but in discreet spots, unlike the foxes whose droppings adorn prominent stones. One of the few forest dwellers active in the daytime is the acrobatic squirrel, easily seen in mid-flight scrambling up the trunk of a pine. The clearest sign of their presence are well-chewed pine cones together with a shower of red scales at the foot of the trees.

In the wake of centuries-long persecution due to fear and ignorance, combined with increasing pressure by man destroying forests and enlarging settlements and pasture, wolves disappeared completely from view in the 1960s. However, sightings of these magnificent creatures are now regular occurrences along the Apennine chain as the population has expanded successfully northwards, recent studies confirming their safe arrival in the Alps. Rather smaller than their North American cousins, the Apennine males weigh in around 25–35kg. Their coat is tawny grey in winter with brown-reddish hues in the summer period. They were afforded official protection as of the 1970s. Stable packs have been reported since the 1980s, aided by the increase in wildlife, and therefore food: wild boar is their favourite prey, though they do not disdain roe deer, sheep and other livestock, for which shepherds receive compensation. Look out for their droppings – dark boar hairs account for the pointy extremity.

Darting lizards such as the eye-catching bright-green variety scuttle through dry leaves, warned off by

Tiny Lago Martini is passed on the way to Passo del Giovarello (Stage 21)

passing walkers. At the opposite end of the speed scale is the ambling but unbelievably dramatic fire salamander, prehistoric in appearance and splashed yellow and black. Long believed capable of passing unharmed through fire, it inhabits beech woods and damp habitats, the females laying their eggs in streams. A rare relative is the so-called 'spectacled' salamander, endemic to the Apennines, and recognisable by yellow-orange patches on its head.

Birds include the omnipresent cuckoo, a constant companion, as well as squawking European jays flying between the treetops, bright blue metallic plumage glinting, sounding the general alarm for other creatures of the woodland. The elusive woodpecker can be heard rat-tat-tatting rather than be seen. Huge grey-black hooded crows are common in fields, as are colourful pheasants which give themselves away with a guttural coughing croak. Nervous ground-nesting partridges take flight from open bracken terrain with an outraged loud, clucking cry.

Birds of prey range from small hawks and kestrels through to magnificent red kites and buzzards, and even the odd stately pair of golden eagles on rocky open ground. But the overwhelming majority are the thousands of 'invisible' songbirds chirping and whistling overhead as you make your way through the woods; early spring is the best time to see them before the trees regain their foliage. In contrast open hillsides are the perfect place to appreciate the skylarks, their melodious inspirational song sheer delight, though more often than not they will be upset by the presence of intruders and make frantic attempts to distract attention from their ground nests. On a warm summer's day huge screeching numbers of house martins, swifts and swallows form clouds around high summits, attracted by the insects conveyed upwards by air currents; they are also commonly seen in villages, as they swoop below eaves and clay-straw nests sheltering their ever-hungry youngsters.

On sunny terrain, especially in the proximity of abandoned shepherds' huts and farmland, snakes may be seen preying on small rodents or lizards. The grey-brown smooth snake, green snake and a fast-moving coal-black type are harmless, though the common viper or adder, light grey with diamond markings, can be dangerous if not given time to slither away to safety. Remember that it will only usually attack if it feels threatened. While not especially numerous, the viper should be taken seriously as a bite can be life-threatening. In the unlikely event that a walker is bitten by a viper (*vipera* in Italian), immobilise the limb with broad bandaging and get medical help as fast as possible – call 118.

At medium altitudes, a postprandial stroll through light woodland on a balmy summer's evening may well be rewarded with the magical sight of fireflies in the undergrowth.

A special mention goes to the humble red wood ant, easily observed in the Abetone forest. They construct enormous conical nests in coniferous forests, which they then protect by devouring damaging parasites. The nests are home to hundreds of thousands of workers which can live up to the venerable age of 10 years, and queens that can survive to the ripe old age of 20!

Last but not least, mention must be made of ticks (*zecche* in Italian). While not exactly in plague proportions, they should not be ignored as the very rare specimen may carry life-threatening Lyme disease. Ticks prefer open areas where grass and shrubs grow and they can attach themselves to warm-blooded animals or walkers. A good rule is to check your body at the end of the day for tiny foreign black spots, an indication they may be gorging themselves on your blood. Remove the creature carefully using tweezers – avoid the temptation to employ a twisting motion, and be sure to get the head out – and disinfect the skin. Recommended precautionary measures include wearing long light-coloured trousers, tucked into socks, and spraying boots, clothing and hat (but not skin!) with an insect repellant containing Permethrin. More information is available at www.lymenet europe.org. Doctors consulted will usually prescribe a course of antibiotics as a precautionary measure. Another line is to keep an eye on the affected skin for a week or so and

Old paved way above Boscolungo (Stage 16)

seek medical advice if any swelling or unusual irritation/itching appears.

PLANTS AND FLOWERS

The plant life in the Apennines is essentially Mediterranean in nature. Generally speaking the southern domains are characterised by Turkey oak and evergreen lentisks with spreads of scrubby maquis, gradually replaced by woodlands of beech, pine and chestnut the further north you go. Beech is predominant from the 900m mark and can be seen growing as high as 1700m. This is a guarantee of memorable colours both in spring with a delicate fresh lime green, then a continuum of vivid reds, oranges and yellows in autumn.

A brilliant contrast is provided by the darker plantations of evergreens, silver fir and spruce. The most memorable forests are to be found in the Casentino (Parco Nazionale delle Foreste Casentinesi), long exploited for shipbuilding: over the 16th to 19th centuries trunks with a minimum girth of 6m and a height of 28m were dragged by teams of oxen to the River Arno and floated via Florence to Pisa to become masts for the navy. In the 1300s timber was also used as scaffolding for Florence's monumental duomo. Lower down, starting at 400m, are spreading chestnut woods, long cultivated as the mainstay of many an Apennine community for both timber and fruit, once dried and ground into nutritious flour.

*Above: Chestnuts litter the ground
in autumn Opposite: Clockwise
from top left: orange lily, lady orchid,
broom, blue gentians, houseleeks*

In the wake of the ice ages the northernmost regions of the Apennines were 'invaded' by alpine plant types in search of warmer conditions, the spruce and alpenrose being typical examples. Walkers will be surprised at the elevated number of alpine flowers on high altitude meadows and grassy ridges. Burgundy-coloured martagon or orange lilies vie for attention with an amazing range of gentians, from the tiny star-shaped variety through to the fat bulbous exemplar and even the more unusual purple gentian, a rich ruby hue. Clumps of pale pink thrift adorn stony ridges. A rarer sight are glorious rich red peonies, while longer-lasting light-blue columbines are another treat on stonier terrain.

Flower buffs will appreciate the delicate endemic rose-pink primrose, which grows on sandstone cliffs in the northern Apennines, and hopefully the less showy but equally rare *Apennine globularia*, a creeping plant with pale-blue flowers. Spring walkers will enjoy the colourful spreads of delicate corydalis blooms, wood anemones, perfect posies of primroses, meadows of violets and the unruly-headed tassel hyacinth. Soon afterwards the predominant bloom is scented broom that covers hillsides with bright splashes of yellow. An unusual prostrate version is Spanish broom, with denser and pricklier growth. May to June is usually the best time for orchid lovers, though it will depend on altitude. There's the relatively common helleborine and early-purple varieties, then the sizeable lady orchid with outspread spotted pink petals resembling a human

23

form, and if you're in luck the exquisite *ophrys* insect orchids.

Bare twigs of mezereon or daphne burst into strongly scented flower in spring, though these morph into bright red poisonous berries at a later stage. Damp marshy zones often feature fluffy cotton grass alongside pretty butterwort, its Latin name *pinguicula* a derivation of 'greasy, fatty' due to the viscosity of its leaves which act as insect traps. Victims are digested over two days, unwittingly supplying the plant with the nitrogen and phosphorous essential for its growth, and which are hard to find in the boggy ambience where it takes root.

Often, the way will be strewn with aromatic herbs – oregano, thyme and wild mint inadvertently crushed by boots scent the air deliciously with pure Mediterranean essences. Grasslands above the tree line are associated with a well-anchored carpet of woody shrubs, notably juniper and bilberry, which spreads to amazing extensions, to the delight of amateur pickers who use them for topping fruit tarts or flavouring grappa.

GETTING THERE

The handiest international airports for the trek start are at Ancona, Pescara, Pisa and Rome, each with ongoing buses and trains. Genoa and Bologna, on the other hand, are closer to the trek conclusion.

Monte Giovo is reflected in the waters of Lago Santo Modenese (Stage 16)

The road pass Bocca Trabaria, where the trek begins, can be reached by bus from either side of the mountainous Apennine ridge thanks to the Baschetti run between Sansepolcro and Pesaro. Otherwise a taxi can come in handy. Pesaro is located on the main Adriatic coast Trenitalia railway line, while Sansepolcro can be reached from Rome via Orte and Perugia thanks to the FCU trains, not to mention Etruria Mobilità bus from Arezzo, which in turn is on the main Florence -Rome railway line.

The trek's conclusion is Passo Due Santi. The closest bus stop is 5km away at the village of Patigno, pick-up point for the ATN bus to the railway station at Pontremoli from where it is easy to travel on to Bologna, Florence or Rome.

See Appendix B for more information and contact details.

LOCAL TRANSPORT

Since time immemorial the Apennines have been criss-crossed by tracks and roads of all sorts linking the Adriatic coast to the Tyrrhenian, and the trek encounters a multitude of road passes and settlements served by public transport. This makes it especially versatile for fitting in with plans for shorter holidays or readjustments on account of unfavourable weather. The capillary bus and train network is reliable and very reasonably priced. Details are given at relevant points during the walk description

and timetables are on display at bus stops and railway stations. Bus tickets should usually be purchased beforehand – at a café, newspaper kiosk or tobacconist in the vicinity of the bus stop – and stamped on board. Where this is not possible just get on and ask the driver, though you may have to pay a small surcharge. The transport company websites are listed in Appendix C and can be consulted for timetables. As regards trains, unless you have a booked seat – in which case your ticket will show a date and time – stamp your ticket in one of the machines on the platform before boarding. Failure to do so can result in a fine.

Useful travel and timetable terminology can be found in Appendix B.

WHEN TO GO

Although the climate in the Apennines is classified as continental, it is subject to the warming influence of the Mediterranean. Summers are generally hot and winters freezing cold. Abundant snowfalls can be expected from December through to March. Thereafter it turns into rain, heavier on the Tyrrhenian side than the Adriatic on account of the moisture-laden winds which blow straight in from the nearby sea.

The GEA was originally designed as a summer itinerary: July–August is the perfect time to go with stable conditions and all accommodation and transport operating. That said, it

Dappled sunlight in springtime woodland

is important to add that – with an eye on hotel/refuge availability – any time from April through to October is both possible and highly recommended. Early springtime can be divine with fresh, crisp air, well ahead of summer's mugginess. It's also a great time to go wildlife watching as the lack of foliage facilitates viewing. Disadvantages at this time of year may include snow cover above the 1500m mark if winter falls have come late, and even the odd flurry, though waterproofs and extra care in navigation can help cope with that.

May usually brings perfect walking weather, neither too hot nor too cold, though some rain is to be expected. Late September–October is simply glorious, with mile after mile

of beech wood at its russet best. On the downside, low-lying cloud and mist are more likely in this season. Encounters with amateur hunters can also be expected in late autumn. Solitary optimists after tiny birds will mostly be camouflaged in hides on ridges and clearings – a polite greeting such as 'Buon giorno' (Good day) is in order to alert them to your presence. The chaotic large-scale boar hunts are not held until the midwinter months.

Walking any later than October will increase the chance of inclement weather and hotel closure. The majority of small towns and villages have one hotel operating year-round, but these sometimes restrict themselves to weekends and public holidays in the off-season. Moreover, with the end of Daylight Saving Time at the end of October the days will be too short for the longer stages.

In terms of transport and accommodation, with the odd exception, it is safe to say that Stages 1–13 are suitable from spring through to autumn, whereas the latter part (Stages 14–23) is limited to midsummer as most higher altitude refuges don't start opening until June.

In terms of Italian public holidays, in addition to the Christmas–New Year period and Easter, people have time off on 6 January, 25 April, 1 May, 2 June, 15 August, 1 November and 8 December. At those times buses are less frequent and accommodation best booked ahead.

ACCOMMODATION

There are plenty of comfortable places to stay along the GEA thanks to an excellent string of family-run hotels (most with en suite bathrooms), alpine-style refuges, walkers' hostels and rooms at monasteries, unfailingly welcoming places at the end of a long day on the trail. These enable walkers to proceed unencumbered by camping gear. Roughly speaking two-thirds of the GEA stages end at a hotel and the remaining third at a refuge. The accommodation options are shown as a yellow house symbol on the sketch maps. All have a restaurant and many offer the *mezza pensione* half board option. Costing around €40–60 per person this includes overnight stay, breakfast and a set three-course

La Verna sanctuary offers accommodation (Stage 3)

dinner (drinks excluded), invariably an excellent deal. Naturally other options such as B&B are also possible. Foodies may prefer to eat à la carte as a greater range of local specialties could be on offer.

Unless otherwise indicated, establishments listed in the route description are open all year round, although off-season can be hit-or-miss as impromptu closures are not unheard of. Whatever time of year you go, don't turn up unannounced but always phone ahead – or book by email where possible – to check there is a free bed and give them time to cater for you. Be aware that mid-August is peak holiday time in Italy and advance reservation is strongly recommended for hot spots such as

Lago Santo Modenese, not to mention rifugi on Saturday evenings in summer, as many put up local walking groups. Lastly, remember that the majority of the road passes are served by buses, enabling you to detour to a nearby village and hotel if need be, an added bonus which gives visitors a rare glimpse into farming communities with vestiges of traditional life.

The *rifugi* (plural of *rifugio*) are marvellous hostel-like huts mostly run by CAI, the Italian Alpine Club, but open to everyone. Reachable only on foot they are manned by a custodian (*gestore*) and a merry band of helpers and provide bunk beds in dormitories, along with a café and restaurant service; most also have hot showers. CAI cardholders and members of

Dinner time at Rifugio Lago Scaffaiolo (Stage 14)

overseas alpine clubs with reciprocal rights are entitled to discounted rates. UK residents can join either CAI or its Austrian counterpart – see Appendix C. A quick note on hut etiquette: walking boots should be left in the entrance hall where slippers or flip-flops are usually available for guests;

Hotel at San Godenzo (Stage 6)

from 10pm to 6am it's 'lights out' and silence. Unless specified otherwise, guests need their own sleeping sheet and towel.

A *Posto Tappa* is the Italian equivalent of the French *gîte d'étape* walkers' hostel; only two are encountered on the GEA – in Stages 7 and 13. They offer dorm accommodation and cooking facilities. Two unmanned and basic *bivacco* huts are also en route – they are always open but you need to be self-sufficient in food, sleeping bag and possibly water. A *foresteria*, on the other hand, refers to guest quarters at a monastery, though these days this usually translates as hotel-standard facilities.

Carry a stash of euros in cash as credit cards are rarely accepted for payment in the rifugi – unlike the majority of hotels and restaurants. Banks and ATMs in villages en route are listed in the walk description.

When using the phone in Italy always include the '0' of the area code, even for local calls. The sole exceptions are toll-free numbers beginning with '800' and mobile phones that start with '3', and the emergency numbers. All attempts at speaking Italian are appreciated – helpful expressions can be found in Appendix B.

Camping

By far the best way to enjoy this trek would be to combine guesthouses and camping out along the way; groceries can be purchased at the villages, and

Rifugio Mariotti sits on the edge of Lago Santo Parmense (Stage 21)

water is available en route. For walkers who prefer the freedom and don't mind the extra weight, the odd discreet pitch won't be a problem. A single night is tolerated in the designated national park areas of the Casentino (Stages 4–6) and the Appenino Toscoemiliano (Stages 18–22). Generally speaking avoid private property and always check where possible. The only designated camping grounds on the route are located near Badia Prataglia (Stage 5), Passo della Futa (Stage 10) and Rigoso (off-route, Stage 20). In any case, early in the season it is a good idea to go equipped with bivvy gear just in case accommodation is not available.

FOOD AND DRINK

Though it stays in Tuscany for the most part, the trek also takes in corners of the Italian regions of Umbria and Emilia-Romagna, and ends up at the doors of Liguria. Each is renowned for distinctive and memorable cuisine, a wonderful bonus for visitors.

A good rule is to be adventurous and ask the staff what their specialities are. Don't skip the antipasti (starters) unless you have a particular aversion to bruschetta, crunchy bread rubbed with fresh garlic, a drizzle of olive oil and chopped fresh tomatoes. Then there are crostini, an unfailingly scrumptious assortment of toasted bread morsels piled with pâté, melted goat's cheese, wild mushrooms or olive paste. Don't miss Emilian crescentine, also known as ficattole by the Tuscans: lightly fried savoury pastry, akin to soft Indian naan bread, served warm with thin slices of ham, salami or local sausage such as finocchiona, flavoured with fennel seeds. The famous cured Parma ham is prosciutto crudo.

All manner of fresh home-rolled pasta is proudly on offer. One traditional speciality is tortelli (similar to ravioli) con ripieno di patate with a potato or zucca pumpkin filling, or stuffed with creamy but light ricotta cheese and spinach. Ravioli toscani on the other hand are filled with meat and vegetables. They come either smothered in rich pomodoro (tomato) or al ragù, the tomatoey-meat sauce that made Bologna famous, if not al burro e salvia (melted butter with a hint of sage). Widespread are pappardelle al cinghiale, flat ribbon pasta served with a rich pungent sauce of stewed boar, not to everyone's taste, though a worthy alternative comes with funghi, wild mushroom sauce. Thick homemade bringoli are a spaghetti lookalike that hail from Umbria and come with sauces of vegetables and mature cheese. Freshly grated parmigiano cheese accompanies most pasta dishes.

Polenta, a thick corn porridge that goes well with stews, may be available; leftover pieces are sometimes fried. Towards the end of the trek near Tuscany's border with Liguria, you'll encounter testaroli al pesto, simple pasta squares prepared from a batter

The Pontremoli valley is clearly seen from Monte Orsaro (Stage 22)

cooked on a griddle, then softened in hot water prior to serving, and accompanied by an aromatic sauce of olive oil, basil, pine nuts, *parmigiano* and *pecorino* cheeses.

Country-style minestrone is a thick flavoursome soup with tons of vegetables, otherwise there's *zuppa di ceci*, chick pea soup, or the traditional home-style Tuscan staple *zuppa di farro* with spelt, a nutty-tasting type of wheat. *Zuppa di porcini* made with mushrooms is a must-taste.

The second course is almost exclusively meat. One standard is the renowned *fiorentina*, a mammoth T-bone steak; the locals boast it has to weigh at least one kilo to earn the name. Then there's lamb which is delicious as crumbed fried cutlets, *agnello*

fritto. Game (*selvaggina*) is common, possibly boar (*cinghiale*), pigeon (*piccione*) or rabbit (*coniglio*). Cheeses are concentrated on the amazing range of tangy *pecorino* from sheep, but there are other cow's milk treats such as rich pungent *formaggio di fosso*, which has been buried in straw and is often served with honey.

Vegetables are usually served as a side dish, *contorno*, and will depend on the season, *verdure di stagione*. An *insalata mista* will get you a mixed salad, with olive oil and vinegar brought separately.

The choice of desserts unfailingly includes *panna cotta*, literally 'cooked cream', and those crisp crunchy *cantucci*, almond biscuits ideal with a glass of sweet amber *vin santo*. You can't go wrong with a *crostata* or tart spread with local bilberries (*mirtilli*) or jam. In many areas where harvesting chestnuts was a traditional mainstay for the economy, you find creamy desserts of *castagne* (chestnuts), cake-like *castagnaccio* and biscuits.

Apart from essential emergency rations (water, biscuits, chocolate and so on), walkers need not weigh themselves down with more than a day's worth of picnic-lunch supplies at a time; even where no shops are encountered, it is normal practice for the rifugi, bar/restaurants and guest-houses to make up a roll (*panino*) with cheese (*con formaggio*), ham (*prosciutto*) or salami. One popular snack typical of the Emilia-Romagna region is the *piadina*, soft home-made flatbread with a filling of ham and cheeses and served grilled (no good for rucksack travel!).

Colazione or breakfast is typically coffee/tea and bread rolls with butter and jam; but if there's the choice it's unfailingly more interesting to take it Italian-style at the local café as a frothy cappuccino or milkier caffè latte with freshly baked pastries or croissants.

On more serious matters, the early Greeks referred to Italy as Oenotria, the 'land of wine'. Ordering *vino della casa* usually results in a drinkable locally produced *rosso* (red) or *bianco* (white). Sangiovese and Trebbiano come from the Adriatic hinterland, then there's always Chianti – the trek starts a matter of kilometres away from the homeland of that nectar. The unique red sparkling Lambrusco hails from the district around Modena in Emilia-Romagna, and comes in a *secco* or dry version as well as *amabile*, verging on sweet. At the end of the GEA you can treat yourself to one of the locally grown Val di Magra wines, which include a refreshing *rosato* or rosé. *Birra* or beer is also widely drunk; *alla spina* means 'draught'. On the liquor front, where available try delicious bilberry-based *mirtillino*, often home-made and served in a tiny glass full of alcohol-impregnated fruit. *Grappa*, the fiery clear aquavit, is often a home-brew infused with wild herbs or fruit such as sultanas.

WHAT TO TAKE

Packing deserves careful thought and preparation as inappropriate or excessive gear can spoil a walking holiday – instead of enjoying those marvellous views you'll be miserable with aching shoulders and blistered feet! Here's a checklist with suggestions:

- comfortable rucksack: when packed pop it on the bathroom scales – 10kg is a reasonable cut-off point
- sturdy walking boots, preferably not brand new and with a good grip sole and ankle support; sandals or lightweight footwear for the evening
- rainproof gear, either a full poncho or jacket, overtrousers and

The beautiful Prataccio cirque (Stage 20)

rucksack cover, depending on personal taste; a lightweight folding umbrella is a godsend for walkers who wear glasses
- layers of clothing to cope with conditions ranging from biting cold winds through to scorching sun: T-shirts, short and long trousers, warm fleece and jacket, woolly hat and gloves, depending on the season
- sun hat, shades, chapstick and extra-high-factor sunblock (remember that the sun's rays become stronger by 10 percent for every 1000m in ascent)
- toiletries and essential medicines
- water bottle
- emergency food: muesli bars, biscuits and chocolate
- walking maps and compass
- whistle for calling for help
- torch or headlamp with new batteries

- trekking poles to ease rucksack weight and aid wonky knees
- sleeping sheet (sleeping-bag liner) and small lightweight towel for refuge stays
- first-aid kit
- camera with recharger
- supply of euros in cash, and credit card
- a supply of plastic bags is handy for organising rucksack contents

MAPS

Walking maps showing details of landscape features, contour lines, road passes and settlements are an essential aid for walkers on this trek. The sketch maps provided in this book give as much detail as possible, and are intended as a guide to show the location of the route with access/exit routes. Due to limitations of space it is not possible to show all landmarks essential for navigation, and sometimes a shortened placename appears on the sketch map, for example Poggio Travi (Poggio delle Travi is used in the route description). Good user-friendly walking maps – *carta escursionistica* in Italian – are published by Kompass and Selca.

Four handy waterproofed Kompass 1:50,000 maps cover the GEA, with the exception of the very start and the final stage.

- Sheet 2459 for Stages 1- 5
- Sheet 2453 for Stages 6–10
- Sheet 2452 for Stages 11–16
- Sheet 2451 for Stages 17–22

Selca does a good series. While not covering the entire trek, the following are helpful:

- Valtiberina e Marca Toscana 1:50,000 for Stages 1–3
- Parco Nazionale delle Foreste Casentinesi 1:25,000 for Stages 4–6
- Alto Appennino Forlivese 1:50,000 for Stages 5–7
- Alto Appennino Imolese 1:50,000 for Stages 8–11
- Alto Appennino Bolognese 1:50,000 for Stages 12–15
- Alto Appennino Modenese 1:25,000 for Stages 15–17
- Parco Nazionale Appennino Tosco-emiliano 1:25,000 for Stages 18–22
- Alto Appennino Parmense est 1:50,000 for Stages 21–22/first part of Stage 23
- Alto Appennino Parmense ovest 1:50,000 for last part of Stage 23

Many maps are available in towns and villages across the Apennines, as well as the occasional local tourist office. Sansepolcro at the very start of the GEA is well supplied. Overseas suppliers include The Map Shop www.themapshop.co.uk at Upton upon Severn, Worcestershire and Stanfords stores in London and Bristol www.stanfords.co.uk; otherwise order from the online bookshop in Florence www.stella-alpina.com.

EMERGENCIES

It is essential to have some form of health insurance. Thanks to reciprocal agreements, members of EU countries only need an EHIC (European Health Insurance Card). Holders are entitled to free or subsidised public emergency care in Italy, which has an excellent health service. UK residents can apply online at www.nhs.uk/ehic. Australia has a similar agreement – see www.humanservices.gov.au. All other nationalities need suitable cover. Travel insurance for a walking holiday is always a good idea as rescue and repatriation costs can be hefty. Members of recognised alpine clubs (see Accommodation above) are usually covered.

Carrying a mobile phone is not necessarily a safety measure as reception is not guaranteed everywhere in the Apennines, valleys included. A whistle – or torch for night times – can be more helpful for attracting attention and calling for assistance.

Mountain Safety

Every mountain walk has its dangers, and those described in this guidebook are no exception. All who walk or climb in the mountains should recognise this and take responsibility for themselves and their companions along the way. The author and publisher have made every effort to ensure that the information contained in this guide was correct when it went to press, but they cannot accept responsibility for any loss, injury or inconvenience sustained by any person using this book.

International Distress Signal *(emergency only)*
Six blasts on a whistle (and flashes with a torch after dark) spaced evenly for one minute, followed by a minute's pause. Repeat until an answer is received. The response is three signals per minute followed by a minute's pause.

Helicopter Rescue
The following signals are used to communicate with a helicopter:

Help required
Raise both arms above head to form a 'Y'

Help not required
Raise one arm above head and extend the other downward, to form the diagonal of an 'N'

Emergency telephone numbers
Italy's all-encompassing emergency phone number is 112.
Ambulance (*ambulanza*) and mountain rescue (*soccorso alpino*) can be contacted on 118.
Forest fires (*incendi boschivi*) should be reported on 1515.
'Help!' is 'Aiuto!' (pronounced 'eye-you-toe').
The code for calling Italy from overseas is +39

Note Mountain rescue can be very expensive – be adequately insured.

On the path near Le Porraie saddle (Stage 18)

However, by all means carry a mobile as when they do work they are also invaluable for coping with unplanned changes in itinerary and practical arrangements.

USING THIS GUIDE

The route has been divided into stages, which correspond to days. Each concludes somewhere with accommodation and meals and often transport. However, individual walkers have their own pace, and stages could be longer or shorter: the route summary table in Appendix A has been provided for this purpose. Intermediate points with facilities such as accommodation and public transport are listed, to make it easier to vary the route.

The information box at the start of each stage contains the following key information:

- **Start** The point at which the day's walk begins.
- **Distance** (in kilometres) This is approximate and nowhere near as significant as ascent/descent.
- **Ascent/descent** Overall height gain and loss in metres (100m = 328ft): the total number of metres the trek climbs and drops during that stage. It is an important indication of effort required and should be taken into consideration alongside difficulty and distance when planning the day. Generally speaking a walker of average fitness will cover 300m in ascent in one hour, although this will be influenced by the gradient and nature of the terrain.
- **Difficulty** Each stage has been classified as follows:
- Grade 1: straightforward walking with little ascent on a forestry track or broad clear path and

problem-free terrain; suitable for first-timers. Corresponds to the Italian 'T' *turistico*.

- Grade 2: moderate difficulty over mountainous terrain or considerable height gain; the equivalent of 'E' *escursionistico*.
- Grade 3: strenuous routes entailing exposed stretches, basic navigation skills preferable. 'EE' *escursionistico esperto*.

It is extremely important to remember that adverse weather increases difficulty. Even a level lane can be treacherous if icy.

- **Walking time** The timings given are approximate and do not include stops for rest, lunch and taking photographs, so always add on a couple of extra hours when planning your day. Midsummer walkers should allow for the inevitably frequent pauses to gather – and consume – the prolific bilberries.

In the route descriptions metres for altitude readings are expressed as 'm' (not to be confused with 'min' for minutes). When 'path' is used it means a narrow pedestrians-only route, whereas a 'lane' or 'track' is a little wider but unsurfaced, and a 'road' is sealed and used by traffic, unless specified differently. Route highlights (corresponding to the sketch map for each stage) are marked in bold in the route description, with altitude and (where relevant) timing for that section of the stage in brackets.

Local path numbering is referred to where relevant, according to the nationwide system of the Italian Alpine Club CAI, with red/white paint stripes and often an identifying number in black. The GEA mostly follows the n.00, sticking to the central Apennine ridgeline. In general waymarking is placed at regular intervals on permanent landscape features such as rocks, though tree trunks are also used, and you will often spot the

A variety of signposts and waymarking is encountered along the trek

GEA logo. Junctions are marked by a clutch of signposts and sometimes a handy green marker column bearing route timings and destinations. (Always take the timings with a generous pinch of salt as they tend towards inaccurate, if not outright wrong.) A plethora of signs denoting different pilgrim ways is now also present on the southernmost stages.

Dos and don'ts

Don't underestimate the Apennines and treat them as a younger sibling of the Alps. There is exciting medium-altitude terrain, but a refreshing lack of summer crowds. Secondly, while elevations are lower than the Alps on the whole, the weather can be fierce. Be aware that the Apennines are prone to surprising extremes, so be prepared. Take weather forecasts seriously and beware any signs of an impending thunderstorm if on a ridge section; use the closest escape route to reach lower, more sheltered, altitudes. Incredibly dense fog can roll in at a moment's notice, obscuring waymarking and transforming a simple path into a high-risk exercise in orienteering. Extremely high winds gusting well over 100kph are not uncommon; keep away from exposed crest routes at all cost as people can be blown off their feet in a trice. Either take a rest day or find a lower level route. If caught out unexpectedly, the recommended technique is to take off your rucksack and lie flat on the ground. As WC Bryant (1835) wrote of the Apennines, 'there the winds no barrier know'!

Read the walk description carefully before setting out, and if

Sunrise at Passo Pradarena (Stage 18)

necessary be prepared to modify your plans to match your level of fitness or fatigue. The GEA is not intended as a marathon route. Plan on reaching your destination in daylight to allow for unforeseen circumstances and give yourself time to recover and make ready for the following day. If in a group, calculate the pace according to the slowest member. It's never a good idea to set out on your own even if you have considerable experience of mountain paths; always tell someone your destination and estimated time of arrival in advance.

Never continue on the trail for more than 10 minutes without checking for route waymarking. If you can't see any, return to the last mark and search from there. A felled tree or new spring growth may have caused the problem.

Be considerate when choosing your stop when nature calls: avoid watercourses and don't leave unsightly toilet paper or tissues lying around. Don't be tempted by rock overhangs or caves, and remember that isolated huts serve as essential shelter for shepherds (and walkers) in bad weather.

Remember that all stock gates should be closed promptly and securely.

English is not widely spoken in the Apennines, but the friendly people always do their utmost to help visitors. Do make an effort to memorise at least basic greetings – see Appendix B.

THE GEA

Alta Via dei Parchi

GEA
Sella del Marmagna 0.45
723
Monte Marmagna 1.00

GEA
Sella Sterpara 0.40
Passo delle Guadine 1.10 719
00 - Monte Brusà 1.40

Lago Padre 0.20
Capanna Braiola 0.50 729
00 - Monte Orsaro 1.45

Lago Santo
(Rif. Mariotti)
1508 m

Signposts at Lago Santo Modenese (Stage 16)

From Passo della Cisa the GEA climbs to the church
of Nostra Signora della Guardia (Stage 23)

The charming town of Sansepolcro

The attractive historic township of Sansepolcro makes a good launching pad for the GEA. It can be reached by Etruria Mobilità bus from Arezzo or FCU train from Rome and has a helpful Tourist Office, plenty of shops and ATMs. It is set in the Valtiberina (Tiber valley), a broad alluvial plain girdled by rising waves of thickly wooded hills cleared in patches for the cultivation of olives and the odd grapevine. The town ostensibly owes its origin to a chapel built by two 10th-century pilgrims to house a relic from the Holy Sepulchre, but is better known to art lovers as the birthplace of 15th-century Renaissance genius Piero della Francesca. Accommodation can be found at Foresteria Santa Maria dei Servi tel 339 6246194 www.santamariadeiservi.it; Hotel Orfeo tel 0575 742287 www.albergoorfeo ristorantedabeppino.com; and Hotel Fiorentino tel 0575 740350 www.albergofiorentino.com. A Baschetti bus links Sansepolcro with the GEA start at Bocca Trabaria; otherwise book a taxi tel 335 5234282.

STAGE 1
Bocca Trabaria to Passo di Viamaggio

Start	Bocca Trabaria
Distance	19km
Total ascent	750m
Total descent	820m
Grade	2
Time	6hr 45min
Note	The stage can be split into shorter sections by overnighting at cosy Pian delle Capanne.

A tiring start to the trek, but exhilarating nonetheless. Narrow paths dodging trees cling to the tight crest, the continuous ups and downs a roller-coaster. Dense woodland is traversed in the company of melodious songbirds and masses of wildflowers; however, the occasional viewpoint over the vast valleys to either side is enjoyed. Trees and rocks alike are resplendent with emerald moss, testifying to the constant mist and low cloud that bring precious moisture to the vegetation.

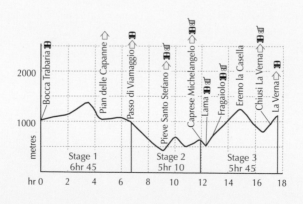

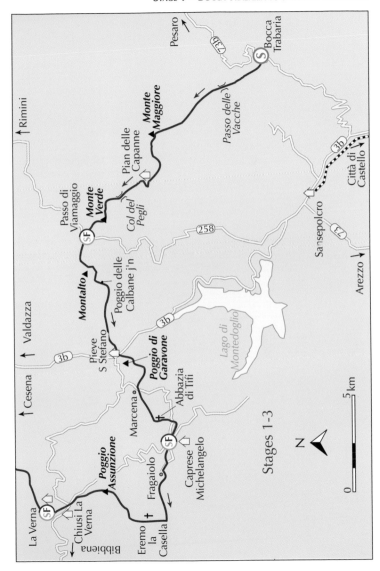

Stages 1-3

Bocca Trabaria is a historic if minor Apennine pass visited by Garibaldi in 1849. Its curious name literally means 'mouth for trunks', because as early as AD500 huge quantities of fir trees from the dense forests along the mountainous crest were being hauled this way by oxen to the River Tiber which flows close to Sansepolcro. Floated downstream to Rome, they were used in the construction of architectural masterpieces such as St Peter's.

From Bocca Trabaria (1049m) the GEA strikes out due W at first, marked regularly with red/white paint stripes and numbered 00. It encounters grassy clearings and lightly wooded ridge with wild pear and apple trees before beech takes over. Occasional gaps in the vegetation afford glimpses southwest to the Valtiberina and its cultivated plain as well as east over rugged hill landscapes. Veering NNW past a string of hunters' platforms, it climbs in fits and starts to Poggio i Tre Termini, a corner of Tuscany's boundary with Umbria and Marche. Close

Misty conditions after Bocca Trabaria

by is **Passo delle Vacche** (1149m, **1hr 20min**) – the 'pass of the cows' – although roe deer are the closest you'll find to a bovine amid the trees; it sports the first of the green column waymarkers.

En route to Monte Maggiore

You continue along the main crest punctuated with stone border markers dating back to 1789, traversing clearings sweet with broom. Keep an eye on waymarks as the path swerves briefly L over the ridge and out of the wood across a grassy slope with great views over Tuscany. Then it's back into woodland punctuated with more hunters' shacks.

At the halfway mark **Monte Maggiore** (1380m, **2hr 10min**), the GEA leaves n.00 to drop L (W) on n.8, 'bull-dozed' by boar diggings further down. After a semi-circular bench the eroded path descends through the Riserva Naturale Alpe della Luna to a dirt road (Monte Cucco Interpoderale, 1025m) where you turn R (NW) for a short leg on a level to **Pian delle Capanne** (1040m, **1hr**) with a picnic area and a newly renovated refuge.

Sleeps 16, bed linen, shower, tel 0575 750000 or 339 6638667, ufficio@thecircle.it, open June–Aug and any time on request. Emergency room always open but no beds.

A muddy lane (n.8b) climbs to coast through open farmland dotted with abandoned buildings, high over Lago di Montedoglio. Gentle descent passes exposed crumbly rock strata to a wide saddle Col del Pegli (990m) where n.00 is joined again. Keep your eyes skinned as the path soon forks R for a remarkably stiff climb due W to **Monte Verde** (1147m) and the reward of superb views. The curious eryngo plant flourishes up here, not far from signposted positions on the Gothic Line.

Now a narrow path drops diagonally R (N), steep and slippery at first. Once over a belvedere knoll, the gradient eases and follows a series of fenced enclosures leading to **Passo di Viamaggio** (983m, **2hr 15min**).

Passo di Viamaggio owes its name to the passage of the Roman road Via Maior. It is surrounded by vast rolling emerald-green upland pasture where sheep and cattle graze.

Etruria Mobilità bus for Sansepolcro, snack bar. The old hotel has closed. Accommodation and meals at La Baita dell'Imperatore, 5km away at Valdazza (tel 0575 790132, info@ristoranteimperatore.it). They have a shuttle service (*navetta* in Italian) for walkers from and to the pass – request this when booking.

STAGE 2

*Passo di Viamaggio to
Caprese Michelangelo*

Start	Passo di Viamaggio
Distance	17.5km
Total ascent	500m
Total descent	850m
Grade	2
Time	5hr 10min

At this point the GEA leaves the main Apennine ridge and its 00 marking for a couple of days to embark on a lovely detour. This stage is especially full and varied and several access/exit points are feasible. Through woodland and farmland, hilltop and valley it leads to charming Caprese Michelangelo, the birthplace of the great Renaissance artist.

▶ At the Y-intersection of roads near Passo di Viamaggio branch L; soon the GEA/n.2 goes L (W) again on an

For route map and profile see Stage 1.

*Descending towards
Pieve Santo Stefano*

unsurfaced road. Forking R (NW) at a house it traverses farmland (close all stock gates as you go), touching on a panoramic knoll with adandoned buildings. Veering below Montalto waymarks lead down to a rough track through light Mediterranean wood and on to a drinking fountain (Fonte delle Rupine). After the **Poggio delle Calbane** junction (800m) a rise is gained before a steep eroded path drops to fields. Keep L (W) at the fork for n.12, soon a stony track back in light woodland but with views over Pieve Santo Stefano. Houses are reached, and you keep L along the banks of the trickling River Tiber (Tevere in Italian) to where a footbridge is crossed into the centre of the modest township of **Pieve Santo Stefano** (431m, **2hr 30min**). ◄

This is the lowest point on the whole of the trek in terms of altitude.

Etruria Mobilità buses to Sansepolcro and Chiusi la Verna, groceries, Hotel Santo Stefano tel 0575 797129 **www.hotelsantostefanoarezzo.it**, accepts credit cards.

Walk straight through to cross the main road and go R then first L over a footbridge. Then narrow Via della Greppa wastes no time in climbing steeply under a motorway. Further up at a farm n.2/GEA veers R as a rocky path in relentless ascent to a conifer plantation on **Poggio di Garavone** (708m).

A lane proceeds SSW straight over the other side and down to a rural hamlet (Stratino basso, 607m). A short stretch of tarmac leads to a fork R (WNW) on n.20, a stony lane through to Casalino hamlet and its dovecotes. At the nearby road and bus stop a lane takes you to **Marcena** (609m). A villa is detoured L and you are plunged into woodland alongside a stream. After a barbed wire gate the way narrows and side streams are easily crossed, then a corridor of broom and juniper shrubs ascends steadily on Poggio Calbeltino. You emerge at a house and minor road. With views across the valley to Caprese Michelangelo, go L downhill to the lovely **Abbazia di Tifi** (530m).

A path plunges through a jungle of brambles to cross a concrete footbridge over a lovely river. A clear path

winding past walnut trees and fields of maize leads up to a road intersection, from where it's a final 1km of tarmac to the prominent knoll that hosts charming **Caprese Michelangelo** (657m, **2hr 40min**).

Arriving at Caprese Michelangelo

> **Michelangelo** was born and christened here in 1475 while his father was serving as chief magistrate, though his mother almost didn't make it after a tiring trip on horseback. Their old house, now a modest museum, is in the Rocca on the cypress-clad hilltop.

> Etruria Mobilità bus, groceries, ATM, a host of marvellous restaurants and Hotel Buca di Michelangelo tel 0575 793921 or 335 8143899 **www.bucadimichel angelo.it**, accepts credit cards.

STAGE 3
Caprese Michelangelo to La Verna

Start	Caprese Michelangelo
Distance	17km
Total ascent	1030m
Total descent	560m
Grade	1–2
Time	5hr 45min

Despite an initial stretch on surfaced if quiet roads, a marvellous day is spent climbing through chestnut wood to a ridge with fine views over extensive forests. Highlights include a peaceful simple chapel retreat, one of the many that hosted St Francis on his travels. Towards the end of the stage is the well-served village of Chiusi La Verna with a choice of hotels, unless you opt to overnight at La Verna, the renowned photogenic Franciscan sanctuary that takes in pilgrims and walkers.

For route map and profile see Stage 1.

◄ From the intersection at the foot of Caprese Michelangelo, head NW downhill on the tarmac. Not far down a signed path short cuts down to a road where you go L through the hamlet of Lama (516m, bus, groceries, restaurant). Keep L up the road (ignore the signs for the overgrown parallel path) for the gentle climb in wide curves to the laid-back hillside village of **Fragaiolo** (714m, **1hr**, Etruria Mobilità bus, café, groceries).

Just above the square is a signed fork – R for Eremo La Casella. Still surfaced it traverses a quiet residential zone and becomes a 4WD lane among magnificent chestnut trees. With the increase in altitude beech takes over, mingled with pine as you head W, crossing the odd side stream. A good way up, a major ridge belonging to Alpe di Catenaia is gained. Here n.50 is joined as you turn R (N) for the final climb to **Eremo La Casella** (1263m, **2hr**). There are marvellous views in

Checking the map at Eremo La Casella

all directions from the picnic area. Modest pale stone chapel and adjoining premises with fireplace and tables, but no beds or water.

A rougher lane (n.50) heads due N in gentle descent through the cover of oak, beech and chestnut. Ahead (due north) your destination the famous Franciscan sanctuary of La Verna is soon visible, set on the lower flank of light grey Monte Penna and overlooking the village of Chiusi La Verna. Views also open up to the east and the main Apennine ridge culminating in Monte dei Frati passed two days back. West below in the Casentino valley are wave upon wave of receding ridges, heavily wooded.

Bearing NE the lane coasts towards Poggio dell'Abete, true to its name 'pine knoll' with a cap of conifers. Keep L but soon afterwards branch R for the path leading N via Poggio Assunzione (1037m). This meanders across grassland bright with a riot of spring wildflowers and unusual concentrations of dog rose and huge juniper bushes. ▸

Bearing NNW you are plunged downhill on a stony path through conifers and across a track and finally

Follow paint splashes carefully.

53

conclude a knee-jarring descent by crossing Torrente Rassina (780m). Scramble up to the road where you go L, but around the corner are pointed R up an old lane. This emerges in a square with a war memorial. Close by is an aged fountain emblazoned with the Campari logo, a hangover from a 1931 publicity campaign. Take the paved lane 'centro storico' parallel to the road for **Chiusi La Verna** (954m, **2hr 15min**).

Park Visitors' Centre, Etruria Mobilità buses to Bibbiena (railway), groceries, an excellent choice of restaurants and homely guesthouses (Da Giovanna tel 0575 599275 **www.dagiovannahotel.com**, accepts credit cards; Letizia tel 0575 599020 **www.hotel-letizia.net**; Bella Vista tel 0575 599029 **www.bellavistalbergo. com**, accepts credit cards).

The old paved way up to the sanctuary of La Verna

Leave Chiusi La Verna on the paved lane alongside Da Giovanna restaurant. Entering the Parco Nazionale delle Foreste Casentinesi, it climbs steadily NNW through pretty woodland brightened with cyclamens. It

winds up to the impressive gateway entrance for the rock stronghold of **La Verna** (1129m, **30min**) on Monte Penna, which has been likened to a raft of limestone afloat on a sea of clay.

Inside La Verna sanctuary

> The capacious Foresteria (tel 0575 5341 **www.sant uariolaverna.org**, accepts credit cards) offers meals and lodging on a par with a hotel.

> The **sanctuary** was founded in 1012 and tradition has it that St Francis received his stigmata here on 14 September 1224. A wander through the lovely premises is recommended and should include a visit to the church for the revered belongings of St Francis as well as the side chapel to admire the 15th-century Della Robbia ceramics, without neglecting the natural gash in the limestone rock where the saint often took rest.

STAGE 4
La Verna to Badia Prataglia

Start	La Verna
Distance	23.5km
Total ascent	575m
Total descent	870m
Grade	2
Time	7hr
Note	An alternative option entails catching a bus via Bibbiena to Badia Prataglia, useful if you need a day off or are interested in visiting the historic towns on the valley floor.

This particularly lengthy traverse lies wholly within the realms of the vast Parco Nazionale delle Foreste Casentinesi. The route returns to the main ridge via farmland, solitary crests and lots of woodland, before finally descending to a well-served village.

Leave La Verna along the paved road out through the sanctuary gates and past car parks and the summer bus stop. After Bar/Ristorante La Melosa the GEA breaks off

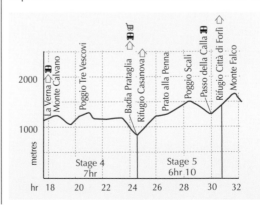

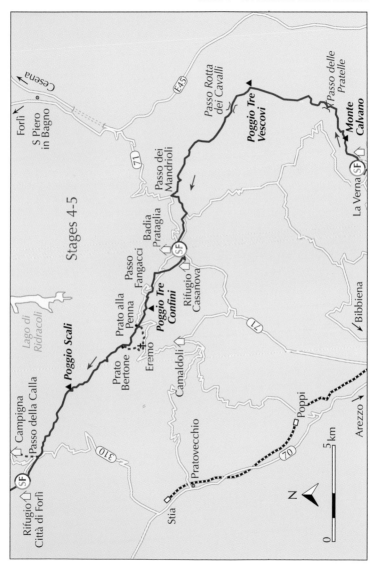

Stages 4-5

L (NE) around the foot of Monte Penna and its towering limestone flanks. From a saddle and a slender wooden cross (Croce della Calla, 1140m), follow n.50 as it strikes off ENE to climb through grass and conifers to **Monte Calvano** (1253m), a favourite with cows and Haflinger horses who enjoy views east over eroded clay ridges referred to as *calanche*.

A muddy lane leads down briefly to key route inter-section **Passo delle Pratelle** (1075m) where you go L (N) for a wonderful level and hugely scenic stretch below Monte Castelsavio and through Passo delle Gualanciole (1040m). Soon the GEA forks R as a path then lane up into the trees. Waymarking is lacking here so follow the green and white signs marking the Riserva Naturale Alta Valle del Tevere. A steep climb ensues to thickly wooded **Poggio Tre Vescovi** (1240m, **3hr**). One of several 'three bishops' mounts' in the region, it sports a green pillar and marks the trek's reunion with the main Apennine ridge and the n.00 route.

After Passo delle Pratelle follow a wide lane

Heading NW now, the narrow path drops quickly through beech, marked by faint paint splashes on tree trunks. After considerable descent it touches on the Buca del Tesoro (1060m), so-named for a treasure trove of Roman coins that came to light there. Further on is **Passo Rotta dei Cavalli** (1173m), a tricky passage for horses. After hunters' hides a 4WD lane is joined. The direction is essentially NW through a sequence of beech, plenty of mud and little in the way of views. Following Passo Montalto (1294m) and conifer forest the way narrows and a drawn-out descent commences. The next recognisable landmark is the narrow road pass of **Passo dei Mandrioli** (1173m, **2hr 50min**), the name a reference to herding.

Here turn sharp L away from the road for the steep descent SW that dodges its way through a wood dominated by soaring pencil-straight conifers and crosses streams, finally reaching a sawmill (812m) and a surfaced road. Turn R downhill past rural properties for the final 2.5km to **Badia Prataglia** (835m, **1hr 10min**). ▶ As you reach the village centre, fork L (sign for the Visitors' Centre) for the hotels.

The Romanesque church is a remnant of the 10th-century Benedictine abbey that gave Badia Prataglia its name.

Etruria Mobilità buses to Bibbiena (railway), Park Visitors' Centre, Arboretum tree park, groceries, bakery, restaurants and hotels (Bosco Verde tel 0575 559017 www.hotelboscoverde.com, accepts credit cards; Albergo Giardino tel 0575 559016 run-down rooms but good restaurant; Pensione La Foresta tel 0575 559009 www.albergolaforesta.eu, accepts credit cards). The best place for walkers is 10min out of the village at Rifugio Casanova – see Stage 5.

STAGE 5
Badia Prataglia to
Rifugio Città di Forlì

Start	Badia Prataglia
Distance	18.5km
Total ascent	1040m
Total descent	430m
Grade	1–2
Time	6hr 10min

This stage follows the main ridge through marvellous tall forest. A short but recommended detour makes its way down to an atmospheric monastic retreat – around 1hr extra. The day concludes at a well-run refuge set in flower-filled meadows that are visited at dusk by deer and wolves. An exit to Campigna for a bus to Forlì is possible.

For route map and profile see Stage 4.

A short way up an old ramp forks R, cutting the corner to the refuge.

◄ From Badia Prataglia walk past Albergo La Foresta to where unsurfaced Via La Casanova breaks off R in gentle ascent away from the village. ◄ After a wide bend is lovely **Rifugio Casanova** (tel 0575 559897 www.rifugionelcasentino.it, always open, cosy rooms and dorms with bathroom, accepts credit cards).

The GEA proceeds uphill on a rough forestry track through oak and conifers to a camping ground and the road with Il Capanno café/restaurant (tel 0575 518015). Opposite, the way continues by sports fields. Proceed uphill as per signs for Fangacci, crossing a nature trail (Sentiero Natura) in a beautiful beech wood. The road is joined, then not far on the GEA branches L (NW), making use of an old paved way in easy ascent through the trees. It emerges at an unsurfaced road and **Passo Fangacci** (1228m, **1hr 30min**), which hopefully won't live up to its name 'muddy pass'.

At Prato alla Penna

Turn L for path n.00 that makes its way W on the edge of a dark conifer plantation on **Poggio Tre Confini**. The climb is gentle, soon passing the Cava dei Frati junction (1358m). Then it's gradually downhill to **Prato alla Penna** (1248m, **40min**) and a minor road pass.

Detour via Eremo di Camaldoli
Keep L in gentle descent WSW on n.74, joining a quiet road on the final leg to **Eremo di Camaldoli** (1103m, **30min**).

> Café, souvenir shop, drinking water, summer Etruria Mobilità bus to Bibbiena and trains. (Should you need year-round buses and accommodation follow signs to Camaldoli – a further 1hr; Hotel dei Baroni tel 0575 556015 www.alberghicamaldoli.it, open Apr–Sept.)

> The name Camaldoli is believed to derive from 'campo amabile' or pleasant field. Set amidst magnificent forest well above its parent monastery in

the lower village, this retreat dates back to 1012. The **Camaldoli order** was founded as an offshoot of the Benedictines. The land was a gift from a count from Arezzo and the monks tended the forest faithfully over the centuries, a task now carried out by the National Park. During opening hours you can peek in to see the row of individual cells akin to bungalows (usually closed 11.30am–3pm).

To return to the GEA, take the marked lane (n.68) along the western perimeter walls. It climbs steadily amidst silver fir then glorious beech, rejoining n.00 at **Prato Bertone** (1330m, **50min**).

From Prato alla Penna continue on the wide track in almost imperceptible ascent NW. Several paths leave the main ridge but you stick to n.00 in the company of squirrels, noisy jays and fallow deer. Wide bends flanked by wild garlic lead uphill and on through a series of grassy clearings, along the edge of the special nature reserve Sasso Fratino. Don't miss the detour R for **Poggio Scali** (1520m, **1hr 50min**), an incredibly panoramic knoll in a sea of wildflowers overlooking grey clay valleys to the north and extensive forests in all other directions. You

Beautiful beech woods en route to Passo della Calla

drop to its foot and a shrine to the Madonna del Fuoco (Our Lady of Fire!). The crest narrows considerably thereafter with continuous wide-reaching views, though the track is broad and clear at all times. Straightforward descent leads through clearings once used by charcoal burners, to **Passo della Calla** (1296m, **1hr 30min**).

> Memorials to World War II partisans, summer Startromagna bus to Campigna, friendly café with delicious home-baked cakes, Rifugio la Calla **www.cai-ss-stia.com** (groups only).

There is an option to leave the GEA here by taking an old route N to Campigna.

Exit to Campigna (40min)
Take the road for Campigna, but after a short stretch of tarmac keep your eyes peeled for a track that breaks off R, revealing lengthy vestiges of the 19th-century paved road, remarkably intact. Further down a lovely cascade precedes **Campigna** (1077m) with a Park Visitors' Centre.

> Startromagna bus to Forlì, Albergo Lo Scoiattolo tel 0543 980052, run by a talented nature photographer, or Granduca tel 0543 980051, which occupies a modest ducal hunting lodge.

At Passo della Calla alongside the café, path n.00 climbs steadily NW through beech. After a ski lift and an old stone refuge building, it emerges on the northeast flank of Monte Gabrendo at La Burraia, an important high-altitude pasture worked until the 1950s and renowned for the butter that gives it its name. This is the location for stunningly positioned, friendly **Rifugio Città di Forlì** (1437m, **40min**).

> Rifugio Città di Forlì tel 0543 980074 or 335 8195234 rifugio@caiforli.it, sleeps 54, open year-round. Memorable dinners and comfortable rooms with bed linen, shared bathrooms.

STAGE 6
*Rifugio Città di Forlì to
Passo del Muraglione*

Start	Rifugio Città di Forlì
Distance	13.5km
Total ascent	470m
Total descent	920m
Grade	2
Time	4hr 30min
Note	Spring walkers can expect late-lying snow on north-facing flanks on the initial high-altitude section.

An incredibly varied day over a fascinating variety of terrain. It begins with a gentle climb to Monte Falco, the highest mountain in the Casentino Park, before a knee-testing descent past a rifugio and through forest to a string of scenic ridges. At Passo del Muraglione there is a choice: a short bus trip down to the village of San Godenzo for a hotel, or walking on for 1hr 30min to find accommodation at welcoming Eremo dei Toschi – see Stage 7.

From Rifugio Città di Forlì at La Burraia, path n.00 climbs diagonally across open grassland alive with skylarks

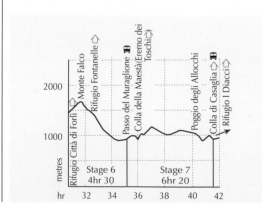

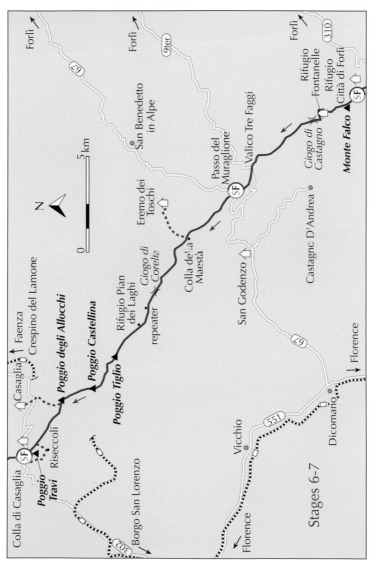

towards the crest to follow a lane R (NNW) into a tunnel of beech with red/white waymarking. You are led along a scenic ridge among springy dwarf mountain pines bursting with songbirds. A cluster of aerials is detoured, a ski lift passed, then a stretch due W concludes at a path junction. Here you leave n.00 temporarily, taking the L branch for the recommended short detour to **Monte Falco** (1657m, **1hr**).

A **special reserve** has been declared here to protect the flora that are rare survivors of the ice age and walkers must not leave the marked paths. The lookout a short way beyond the summit enjoys sweeping views in clear weather, taking in the curious strata of the Balze di Rondinaia.

Back at the junction resume n.00 for the constant descent N through wood to an unsurfaced road at Passo Piancancelli (1500m, **30min**). Keep straight over for a path threading its way through dense beech wood. About 10min along fork L downhill in descent (mostly N) to emerge on a forestry track amid conifers. A short way along L will see you at **Rifugio Fontanelle** (1389m, **30min**).

Rifugio Fontanelle tel 338 3269011 **www.rifugio fontanelle.it**, open mid-June–mid-Sept, basic hut with dorms. Booking essential. Emergency room always open but no beds.

A clear path heads W and you're quickly plunging downhill to see the light of day once more on a delightful scenic ridge with lovely view south to a waterfall, while below is a divine green valley with scattered farms. Not far down n.00 turns L onto a good forestry track and gains open hillside and the broad saddle of **Giogo di Castagno**, also known as Passo del Giogo (1082m, **45min**). Well-placed benches invite walkers to enjoy the panorama that takes in the twin peaks of Falco and Falterona, as well as the village of San Godenzo west-northwest in a sea of green.

About 20min along on Poggio Piano (1108m) you break L off for a brilliantly panoramic if narrow path NNW through light wood. The Park border is followed then the track rejoined to climb a modest knoll thick with broom, not far from **Valico Tre Faggi** (989m, **1hr**), a minor road pass. ▸

Now it's NW for a matter of minutes; keep L at a fork for a pretty scenic stretch across dry terrain with Mediterranean herbs and shrubs, not to mention an infinity of lizards. A couple of slightly exposed passages are encountered, slippery in wet conditions.

For a **straightforward alternative** to avoid the tricky stretch, ignore the aforementioned fork and take the next L just before a vehicle barrier. There's no signpost, but 00 on trees. It climbs a tad and has a lovely outlook, before a final plunge to the pass.

You finally coast in to **Passo del Muraglione** (907m, **45min**) so-named for the ponderous elongated masonry

On the way to Valico Tre Faggi with vast views over the Mugello

The name 'three beeches pass' is presumably tongue-in-cheek in view of the abundance of trees!

wall dating back to the 1830s, designed to prevent carriages from overturning in the strong winds that characterise the Apennines.

The pass is incredibly popular with motorcyclists – as you'll discover for yourself if you happen through on a weekend or bank holiday. Couple of bar/restaurants with draught beer and delicious toasted piadine snacks.

For your overnight stop, consider pushing on a further 1hr 30min to Eremo dei Toschi – see Stage 7. Otherwise take the late afternoon AMV bus west down to San Godenzo. An early morning run will deposit you back at the pass the next day, except Sunday and hols, when the hotels will find you a lift.

The charming village of San Godenzo

Romanesque abbey, ATM, groceries and two excellent restaurant-hotels, Albergo Agnoletti tel 055 8374016 or Lo Chalet tel 055 8374043 or 335 7898128; bus to Dicomano station and connections to Florence.

STAGE 7

Passo del Muraglione to Colla di Casaglia

Start	Passo del Muraglione
Distance	23km
Total ascent	700m
Total descent	700m
Grade	2
Time	6hr 20min
Note	The stage mostly coincides with the SOFT (Sorgenti di Firenze Trekking) denoted by yellow waymarking (as well as the usual red/white stripes).

Today you turn your back on the heavily forested Falterona-Falco group and the National Park to head into more modest and quieter hilly ranges. This lengthy stage leads through lightly wooded terrain meticulously following narrow crests. There is no respite from ascents and descents, and no intermediate stopovers. It is perfect for lovers of solitude and there are plenty of views over rolling countryside. En route is a short detour for lovely Eremo dei Toschi, an alternative place to stay. At day's end, either drop to the village of Casaglia and the walker's hostel or stay at the modest hotel at the road pass.

▶ Behind the cafés at Passo del Muraglione a sign for the Sorgenti di Firenze Trekking (SOFT) points you up path n.00 leading NW along the wooded ridge thronging with squirrels and brightened by cyclamens. There is a neat separation between beech and fir, while clearings have been colonised by broom and bracken. Half an hour along at a track you dogleg L then R, soon dropping to a wide gravel lane. Not far along path n.00 strikes uphill through a zone frequented by hunters to **Colla della Maestà** (1009m, **1hr 10min**), with a column marking an intersection of unsealed roads.

For route map and profile see Stage 6.

Ups and downs are the flavour of this stage

To detour to **Eremo dei Toschi**, also known as Santa Maria (20min) fork R for Aquacheta and further on follow signs for the Eremo. The former hermitage has been converted into an agriturismo by a young family. Lovely rooms (bed linen provided) with showers, and simple meals tel 340 3258726 sebula@lamiamail.net.

Continue along the lane/n.00 NW at first. In addition to beech woods here are cultivated fields and pasture, the going persistently up and down. After following a fence, go straight across a saddle and waymarks reappear in the trees. Further on, look out for the yellow poles of a gas pipeline (*metanodotto*). Its access track is used briefly but take care not to miss the resumption of n.00 back in woodland L. Not far on is the saddle **Giogo di Corella** (1137m), identifiable by a green column and turn-off for Corella. Continue through beech wood, soon veering R in rough descent on a sunken path to emerge on open hillside studded with orchids. There are lovely views over the patchwork of farmland in fertile Val di Sieve southwest.

After a huge telecommunications **repeater** (easily mistaken for a cinema screen!), an increasingly panoramic lane leads gently uphill to a hunters' hut **Rifugio Pian dei Laghi** (no facilities for walkers). A knoll in a vast sea of bracken and asphodels is followed by more huts and **Poggio Tiglio**. Then ignore a turn-off for Crespino before **Poggio Castellina** (1306m) whose hawthorn-clad slopes regale views to the snow-spattered northern Apennines. Take care not to miss the sharp turn R which eventually reaches the eroded but lovely open pasture of **Poggio degli Allocchi** (1019m, **3hr 50min**) 'knoll of the owls' (also the branch for Casaglia with a view north to the village).

Path to Casaglia (1hr)

A signed branch (GEA) R heads decidedly downhill to the road and Casaglia (754m), which has groceries and a Posto Tappa (tel 055 8402810 or 339 8740786 with basic dorm accommodation for 20 and the use of a kitchen). The railway station of Crespino del Lamone (on the Florence–Faenza line) is only a few kilometres downhill, and there are buses.

To rejoin the GEA, head uphill to Monte La Faggetta – at least 1hr – and pick up the route description from Stage 8.

From Poggio degli Allocchi continue straight along the broad crest to dip via a saddle and straight up the other side on an overgrown path WNW. Push your way up to the edge of a conifer plantation, and bear L. A lane is joined through beech to a signed junction: though waymarks veer L here, the most direct route goes straight ahead and past a traffic barrier. It cuts through a logging area before dropping to the road pass of Colla di Casaglia.

The **'official' route** is 30min longer: from Poggio degli Allocchi turn L to skirt Poggio delle Travi as far as the crumbling stone houses of Riseccoli. Here it's sharp R climbing on a wider track. Some 10min

Colla di Casaglia, where the stage concludes

up, watch out for a lane R (n.34–00) up again on a muddy rutted way over a rise. It finally descends and is joined by the direct route on the home run.

The stage ends at **Colla di Casaglia** (913m, **1hr 20min**), not to be confused with Passo della Calla.

In late spring the pass is witness to the all-night Florence-Faenza ultra marathon, known as **Il Passatore**, to commemorate the best known of the Apennine bandits, a 19th-century Robin Hood and patriot.

Locanda della Colla tel 055 8405013, accepts credit cards, guesthouse (shared bathrooms) and restaurant that does memorable crostini and grilled meat. As photos in the bar show, the surrounding slopes were surprisingly bare until reforestation in the 1960s. The occasional AMV bus runs to Borgo San Lorenzo for trains.

STAGE 8

*Colla di Casaglia to
Badia Moscheta*

Start	Colla di Casaglia
Distance	19.25km
Total ascent	450m
Total descent	800m
Grade	1–2
Time	5hr 45min
Note	A shorter direct route missing out Badia Moscheta is given as an alternative; it rejoins the GEA in Stage 9. On the other hand, it is feasible to combine Stages 8 and 9 but make an early start as it will take 7hr 55min.

This loop detours temporarily off the main Apennine ridge via scenic ridges and concludes with an attractive steep-sided river valley and a delightful converted monastery. Walking is leisurely on mostly clear lanes and forestry tracks. A short detour can be made to a lovely refuge if desired.

Direct route to Passo del Giogo (3hr 30min)

From Colla di Casaglia take the Palazzuolo sul Senio road for 1.5km to a bend where n.00, a forestry lane, breaks off

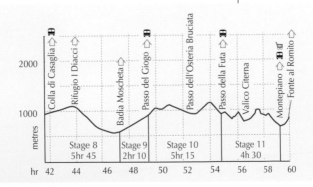

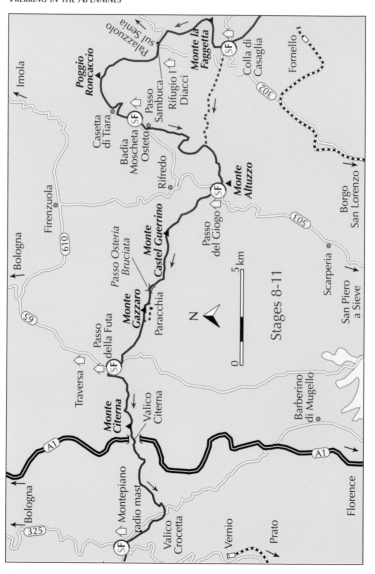

Stages 8-11

L (WNW). Coasting around the 1000m mark, it touches on a clearing with Capanna Marcone (always open, emergency shelter only). Panoramic points with benches dot the way. A fork R for Badia Moscheta is ignored, and the lane skirts the northern flanks of Monte Pratone. Further on it is joined by the GEA as it climbs from Osteto, for the final 1hr together to **Passo del Giogo** (see Stage 9).

From Colla di Casaglia, head out on the surfaced road for Palazzuolo sul Senio for a couple of minutes until path n.505 takes you climbing steeply R (its final destination is the renowned ceramic city of Faenza, 16hr away!). At a ridge dark with conifers, it veers R (E then NE) and becomes a clear track through beech wood. Soon after a spring on aptly named Monte La Faggetta ('beech wood mount'), is the link with the variant from Casaglia (see Stage 7).

Path n.505 now heads up to a lovely lookout point and proceeds N, but you part ways further along as it turns decidedly R (E) and the GEA drops to a minor saddle (Passo Ronchi di Berna, 1103m). Here, on the R side of the ridge with vestiges of an old road, you descend gently to a huge cross on the roadside. Within view of impressive grey stratified mountainsides head L up the road beneath Monte Carzolano the short distance to **Passo Sambuca** (1080m, **2hr**). ▶

You need the lane (n.701) on the southern side of the pass. In gradual ascent W it passes a turn-off for **Rifugio I Diacci** (tel 055 0763031 or 339 7722208 www. rifugimugello.it, open Aug and weekends, booking essential) and leads to a wonderfully open crest amid farmland and a key junction with two variants: L via Val di Rovigo is marginally shorter but is less scenic as it follows a deep-cut valley. Your route R (N) sticks to the 4WD track (n.701), cruising high above the wild valley. A good 1hr along the wood begins to thin in the proximity of a photogenic ruined house and GEA waymarking points you L beneath **Poggio Roncaccio**.

Here there is a monument to partisans active during World War II.

A rough farm track dips W below eroding grey terraces past a string of abandoned farms and there are views N to quarries gashed out of mountainsides. Prosperous chestnut plantations announce the proximity of the tiny hamlet of **Casetta di Tiara** (650m, **2hr**) in a world of its own (cool church, drinking water, scented lilac bushes, café-restaurant).

To the L of the church a narrow path plunges S past a clutch of houses then straight down to the watercourse, old mill and footbridge in pretty Val di Rovigo. Then it's decidedly R (W) along a lane for 10min to a bridge (car park on the opposite bank and road to Firenzuola). Don't cross over but keep on the clear if narrow path (n.713) S along the L bank of the Veccione. Climbing a little through cool woodland it enters Val d'Inferno (hell valley), far from roads and civilisation. Further ahead the valley narrows and you pass high above the cascading torrent that flows below towering grey sandstone cliffs, home to birds of prey. Inviting green pools are accessible at several points for a dip. A final climb leads out to a minor road where L it's a matter of minutes to a well-earned cool beer at **Badia Moscheta** (569m, **1hr 45min**).

St Peter and the porcupine at the abbey at Badia Moscheta

The restaurant at Badia Moscheta

The finish point of Stage 8 is justifiably popular at weekends and holidays, but a haven of peace at other times. The **abbey**, which dates back to 1040 and bears the emblem of St Peter and a porcupine, was home to a religious order until 1784.

The converted monastery houses a museum, whereas lovely rooms and dorms with bathroom are located in modern buildings. Tel 055 8144015 **www.bad iadimoscheta.it**, accepts credit cards, open mid-Mar–mid-Nov, friendly home-style restaurant with T-bone steaks and luscious pasta. AMV bus 3km away at Rifredo on the road to Firenzuola.

STAGE 9
Badia Moscheta to
Passo del Giogo

Start	Badia Moscheta
Distance	8km
Total ascent	300m
Total descent	0m
Grade	1–2
Time	2hr 10min

This is a short, semi-rest day, handy in view of the lengthy stage that follows. In the vicinity of Passo del Giogo you can always make an interesting side trip to Monte Altuzzo to explore positions on the World War II Gothic Line.

For route map and profile see Stage 8.

◀ Leave Badia Moscheta past the stables along the road SW. It's only 10min to the branch L for the peaceful hamlet of **Osteto** (583m, café). Uphill an ancient chestnut wood is traversed and the path heads S accompanied by a gurgling stream. Wide curves climb through the abandoned terraces and orchards of Pratelle to emerald meadows. Up at a fence with a marker column, the lane and direct route from Colla di Casaglia is joined (see Stage 8). Heading SW now, you wind up to shady woodland for a leisurely traverse with sweeping views over patchwork farmland surrounding the township of Firenzuola.

Marked 'Sentiero della Linea Gotica', a path branches off to **Monte Altuzzo**, a key position on the Gothic Line of German defence during the Allied advance up Italy at the end of World War II. Follow the marked path for the loop walk illustrated with information boards (1hr 30min).

The stage ends at **Passo del Giogo** (882m, **2hr 10min**), also known as Giogo di Scarperia.

AMV buses to Firenzuola or San Piero a Sieve, hotel/restaurant Al Giogo tel 055 8468320 or 335 7495602 **www.passodelgiogo.it**, accepts credit cards.

The old path above Osteto

STAGE 10
*Passo del Giogo to
Passo della Futa*

Start	Passo del Giogo
Distance	13.5km
Total ascent	600m
Total descent	580m
Grade	2–3
Time	5hr 15min

This stage is taxing to say the least as the path follows the narrow crest religiously. Each time you puff up to a knoll and start getting your breath back, you find yourself heading straight down the other side in a knee-testing drop! Walking is on a mix of clear paths and straightforward forestry tracks. During the latter part it is possible to opt for a lower, easier (Grade 2) route, 15min shorter, detouring Monte Gazzaro (Grade 3). Accommodation at day's end is at a camping ground (with bungalows) or a comfortable hotel 2km away.

For route map and profile see Stage 8.

◄ At Passo del Giogo a track leads alongside the buildings, soon swinging NNW to a great panoramic ridge dominating the fertile Mugello alluvial plain. As the vegetation alternates between beech, fir, oak and hawthorn the narrow path makes its way along the knobbly ridge relentlessly ascending and descending. Bearing NW is a particularly steep climb to 1117m **Monte Castel Guerrino**. Thereafter n.00 becomes a rough wider track, passing a turn-off for Sant'Agata. The next useful landmark is a radio mast and soon an inviting hut with its own meadow, a perfect picnic spot. Not far on at a saddle and 1824 boundary stone, keep on down to nearby **Passo dell'Osteria Bruciata** (920m, **3hr**) and a huge triangular marker.

En route to Osteria Bruciata

'Burnt Inn Pass' earned its name in medieval times. Pilgrims would take shelter there, but when guests started to disappear and the innkeeper served meat dishes the next day…the locals put two and two together, ganged up and burnt the premises to the ground.

If at this point you've had your fill of slippery ups and downs, then opt for the easier lower route.

Lower route via Paracchia
Ignore the lane for Sant'Agata and go diagonally W down the rough track past an empty stone building (**Paracchia**, 897m). Stick to the muddy lane (n.50) traversing undulating terrain beneath a grey terraced outcrop. Around 30min from the pass fork R (NNW, 919m) climbing through beech once more. Logging work in the wood can make the going muddy. You skirt **Monte Gazzaro**, rejoining the main GEA in another 30min.

The ascent to Monte Gazzaro

Walkers with energy to spare and an unquenched thirst for vast views should brace themselves for stiffer climbs and embark on path n.00 NE over Il Poggiolino to slopes thick with wildflowers. More steep ascent culminates at a brief detour for a Punto Panoramico (lookout). Then it's not far to a huge cross and radio mast on **Monte Gazzaro** (1125m) which boasts almost 360° views including snow-spattered Corno alle Scale in the distance west. A line of concrete poles leads down to join the lower route.

Keep straight ahead WNW for the day's final ups and downs, then descend gradually on a rutted lane to the roadside. Go L and immediately R through a busy round-about. Take the Traversa road to reach nearby **Passo della Futa** (903m, **2hr 15min**) café-restaurant (no rooms). AMV buses to Florence, also connections for Bologna.

A 10min walk uphill (signposted – see Stage 11) is a nicely positioned campsite. Camping 'La Futa' tel 055 815297 or 328 9248746 **www.campinglafuta. it** is open mid-Apr–Nov with self-catering bungalows

The war cemetery at Passo della Futa

with en suites and a restaurant. Otherwise a hotel/restaurant and groceries can be found 2km north of Passo della Futa at Traversa: Albergo Jolanda tel 055 815265, accepts credit cards (bus or walk).

Above Passo della Futa is a poignant **war cemetery** where over 30,000 German soldiers from the 1939–45 conflict were laid to rest. The largest burial ground of its type on Italian soil, it was inaugurated in 1969 and is tended by a volunteer group; additions are occasionally made as sad discoveries come to light in woods and fields. The Gothic Line ran through here and the ridges and hilltops for miles around were cleared of vegetation for defence purposes in view of the advancing Allied forces. The positions fell in September 1944.

STAGE 11

*Passo della Futa to
Montepiano*

Start	Passo della Futa
Distance	14.5km
Total ascent	420m
Total descent	620m
Grade	2
Time	4hr 30min

Today the trek crosses one of Italy's busiest motorways, the Autostrada del Sole. However, as this burrows deep through the Apennines, emerging only occasionally for air, the presence of traffic is limited to a distant rumble. The GEA keeps well above it by crossing Monte Citerna where an abrupt descent is followed by a series of quiet paths and logging tracks. The day concludes on a pretty woodland route to the lovely, well-served hill village of Montepiano.

For route map and profile see Stage 8.

◀ From the café-restaurant at Passo della Futa take the path cutting up towards the war cemetery entrance, where red/white marking points R up the road. Not far on, at the rear of the premises, the GEA/n.00 forks L passing close to Camping La Futa. Soon you join a quiet abandoned surfaced road, the tarmac cracked and colonised by scented dog roses. Half an hour on, the GEA forks R as a path in ascent to the lovely wooded ridge of **Monte Citerna**, albeit detouring the actual 958m top. The motorway is glimpsed in the distance through the trees. Overgrown tracts and a knee-testing descent conclude at a lane that drops to **Valico Citerna** (781m, **1hr 45min**) directly over a motorway tunnel – though you wouldn't know it as it's so peaceful up here. Go straight up the other side past a rusty gate, then sharp R (W) into beech woodland where a stream is crossed three times in succession. Up at a lane, branch R to abandoned houses (Rifiletti, 886m). Keep L here on a forestry track and on through a seven-way junction. ▸ Not far on are vast pine forests, imbued with resin scent and pink filtered light. Wide curves descend through a logging zone past a derelict building (Poggio dei Prati) and to **Valico Crocetta** (817m, **1hr 45min**), a minor road.

The traffic noise has completely faded away now and birdsong takes over.

Go briefly R then sharp L for the gentle climb on n.00 to a wooded crest heading N. The clear path meanders through to a radio mast on a knoll, where you turn L on the concrete ramp track. Not far down near a gate, you're pointed R for the final leg to the peaceful verdant basin housing **Montepiano** (700m, **1hr**). At the road, stroll L beneath lime trees to helpful Hotel Margherita (tel 0574 959926 www.margheritahotel.com, accepts credit cards). Just around the corner after the war memorial (on Via della Badia) is Ca' del Setta (tel 0574 959829 or 329 8250430 www.cadelsetta.it).

Montepiano nestles in a green valley

The war memorial at Montepiano

Montepiano is popular with summer holidaymakers and also acts as a key centre for the winter boar hunts, as is obvious from the gruesome tusked heads on display. You're hard put to imagine that the high-speed Bologna–Florence railway tunnel runs directly beneath the village. ATM, groceries, CAP buses to San Quirico di Vernio for trains to Prato or Bologna.

STAGE 12

Montepiano to Rifugio Pacini

Start	Montepiano
Distance	17km
Total ascent	850m
Total descent	550m
Grade	2
Time	5hr 15min

A divine stage leading through a wonderful never-ending sea of herringbone crests cloaked in thick woodland 'infested' with deer and dotted with evocative wayside shrines and thirst-quenching springs. You're miles away from it all, circling high above the Bisenzio valley that runs down to the textile town of Prato.

Leave the village of Montepiano by turning R (due W) on the road Via della Badia (GEA/n.23 marker), a divine avenue past a small lake and bar/pizzeria. Keep on up

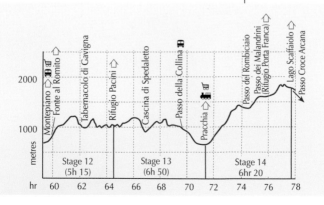

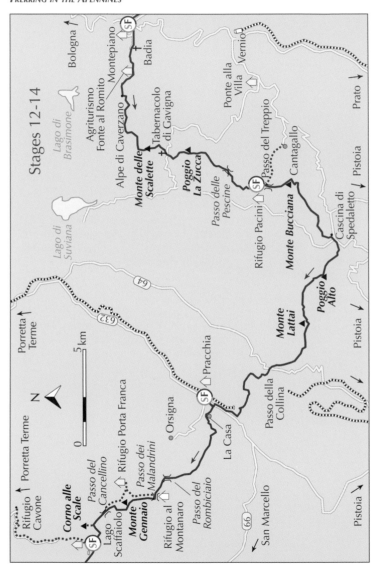

Stages 12-14

through the tranquil hamlet of **Badia**, which boasts a 12th-century monastery with an exquisite Romanesque portal. On a rougher partially surfaced road continue through mixed wood to **Agriturismo Fonte al Romito** (tel 0574 959468 or 338 5036368, only open for groups).

At the rear of the buildings fork R on the rough track that launches on a steep ascent NW, soon becoming a path. The wood thins as you climb through meadows covered in orchids and flowering thyme, and dotted with hunters' hides. A welcome spring Fonte del Canapale (950m) precedes a hut where you need to keep straight ahead to a broad white lane. Turn L through the **Alpe di Caverzano** (1008m, **1hr 20min**), the summer quarters for dwellers of the eponymous lower village; well-tended vegetable gardens are very much in evidence.

At a shrine and waymark column, the GEA/00 breaks off R (NW) via a lane then a path L for more ascent to a tabernacle in woodland. In the company of old stone markers you follow the edge of the Parco Regionale Laghi di Suviana e Brasimone. A gentle climb ensues to vast

Via della Badia at Montepiano

89

A gap in the trees gives a vast outlook

expanses of broom and bracken and a ridge on **Monte delle Scalette** (1186m) with a vast outlook where you're hard put to pinpoint a settlement in the endless sea of green. Via a saddle you plunge past crumbling rock layers to a scenic corner dominating the village of Fossato gathered on a narrow ridge. Gentler descent S concludes at the minor road pass of **Tabernacolo di Gavigna** (968m, **1hr 40min**) and a huge shrine-cum-chapel. ◄

Some thoughtful soul has fitted the chapel out with settees to the delight of footsore walkers!

An inevitable stiff but shady climb takes you S to the 1139m mark on **Poggio La Zucca**, but before you have time to enjoy it, the path descends again. A huge pylon spells wide-ranging views both sides of the ridge. Further on at **Passo delle Pescine**, with a shrine bearing a colourful ceramic Madonna, the GEA does an abrupt swerve R (SW) to the moss-ridden Fonte di Pluto spring. You soon cross a surfaced road and follow signs into the wood for the short remaining stretch to Pian della Rasa. Here stands modernised and well-run **Rifugio Pacini** (1001m, **2hr 15min**).

Rifugio Pacini tel 366 8985418 or 3498057163 pacinirifugio@gmail.com CAI, sleeps 22, shower, open Apr–Nov weekends and whenever requested (phone or drop them an email). Emergency room sleeps 2.

STAGE 13
Rifugio Pacini to Pracchia

Start	Rifugio Pacini
Distance	24.25km
Total ascent	600m
Total descent	960m
Grade	2
Time	6hr 50min
Note	Soon after Rifugio Pacini a handy exit route leads to Cantagallo (accommodation and transport).

This longish stage commences with a beautiful wander through more beech woodland, home to deer and boar and dotted with charcoal burners' clearings. The GEA then heads over a string of knolls before calling in at a tiny village with a café-restaurant and a bus service. The concluding leg heads down to the verdant Reno river valley where a modest village awaits with good facilities and a train line.

▶ From Rifugio Pacini a short stroll S through the wood will see you at **Passo del Treppio** (996m).

For route map and profile see Stage 12.

Exit to Cantagallo (1hr)
From Passo del Treppio n.50 drops steadily ESE in the company of roe deer to a brief stretch of road then path to **Cantagallo** (572m).

> The rural community of 'cock crow', as the name goes, boasts a minuscule café and CAP bus service to Vernio for trains to Prato or Bologna. Otherwise 4km downhill is Agriturismo Ponte alla Villa tel 0574 956244 **www. ponteallavilla.com** with accommodation, meals and pick-up from Cantagallo.

The main GEA route continues S from Passo del Treppio past turn-offs to where n.00 bears R over a rise past a

Strolling through the woods on the way to Cascina di Spedaletto

forestry authority plantation. Then it's a coast SE around the east flank of **Monte Bucciana** to Fonte Fonterabbi (picnic tables). Further on is a simple wooden cross marking the grave of a German soldier. At a tiny cabinet shrine, leave n.00 to fork R on n.13. Further along this plunges through deep leaf litter to a lovely picnic meadow shaded by gigantic beeches at **Cascina di Spedaletto** (881m, **2hr 15min**), originally a 12th-century hospice.

Take the road (marked n.00) directly opposite the Cascina's access lane. This goes SW to cross a larger road where you head uphill on a good forestry track. After 20min of shady ascent n.00 forks abruptly R (NW), with views to the sprawling town of Pistoia. It's a steady climb to a wooded crest thick with bilberries and swathes of broom, and inspiring views north into the Limentra valley. After **Poggio Alto** (1093m) and a clearing with huts, follow a surfaced road L to a saddle and fork R on a path up through conifers. The road is touched on further ahead at a traffic barrier where you embark on a steep ascent on a faint path. Keep over the top of **Monte Lattai** (1141m) and down the other side to a house in a meadow where the road is rejoined.

Not far along after bar/pizzeria La Baita del Termine, the GEA branches R on a rough lane that soon begins a descent down a stony way to the road and the cluster of old stone houses and pleasant surrounds of **Passo della Collina** (932m, **2hr 50min**) bar/restaurant. CAP buses to Pistoia and Porretta Terme (railway).

Take the narrow road signed for Pracchia. After the last house keep L on a surfaced road with faded way-marks. At a bend the GEA goes R as a lane flanking fenced enclosures for training hunting dogs (*addestramento cani da caccia*). Gentle uphill leads past hunters' shacks and a fork for a *quagliodromo* (quail) hunting arena on Poggio Lagoni. Walk straight on through a traffic barrier to a sharp L turn across a meadow frequented by boars and on to the flowered rocky saddle Piastreta (897m). Path n.33 leads mostly N in easy descent to join a disused road L past a concrete bunker left over from World War II. This drops to the tranquil green Reno valley via a restored landslide site. After a playing field and a mineral-water bottling plant, the road dips under the railway line; turn R past a war memorial and beneath lilac and horse chest-nut trees to **Pracchia** (635m, **1hr 45min**) in a quiet steep-sided valley, whose sunless depths in winter were once exploited for ice production.

Hotel Melini tel 0573 490026 **www.albergomelini. com**, accepts credit cards, with spotlessly clean rooms and inspirational restaurant, extends a warm welcome to walkers. Otherwise dorm accommodation for 25 available at the nearby Posto Tappa tel 0573 1935245 or proloco.pracchia@prolocopracchia.it, shower, kitchen, local restaurant. The village also has groceries, ATM and a railway station on the scenic single-track Pistoia–Porretta Terme line with connections to Bologna.

STAGE 14

Pracchia to Lago Scaffaiolo

Start	Pracchia
Distance	16km
Total ascent	1450m
Total descent	300m
Grade	2–3
Time	6hr 20min
Note	The day's load can be split into more manageable sections by overnighting at welcoming Rifugio Porta Franca accessibile via a short detour.

This stage marks an exciting change in geography and scenery for the GEA. With the increase in altitude, the thickly wooded hillsides of the past weeks are gradually left behind and dramatic bare crests with marvellous far-reaching views become the flavour of the day. Conditions verge on alpine in many places and steepness is constant. A lengthy but superbly varied haul – and a must-do Apennine peak.

For route map and profile see Stage 12.

◄ From Pracchia return along the road (Pistoia direction) past the war memorial to where the GEA/n.33 forks R to cross the Reno river on a footbridge. It then puffs up a narrow road to a curve and a house – don't miss the pylon turn-off R up through wood to a minor road and **La Casa** (790m, 30min) a sleepy hamlet crowned by productive cherry trees.

Waymarks point you up through the houses to a shrine where the GEA goes sharp L (WSW) for unrelenting zigzags to gain the wooded ridge. There's only a brief level respite before the path resumes its uphill trend bearing NW through magical woodland, a state forest, with glimpses of the underlying Orsigna valley. Apart from several path forks, the first useful landmark – and sign that the bulk of the ascent is behind you – is a picnic table in a shady clearing Pian della

Trave (1317m), 'plain of the beam', a reference to the timber industry.

The River Reno is crossed at the start of the stage

The lovely ensuing stretch (n.33) entails relatively little climbing, so there's time to enjoy the divine beech trees, grey-trunked, tall and straight, and the magical plays of dappling light. After a disused ski lift you coast N to **Passo del Rombiciaio** (1362m, **2hr 40min**, picnic table). ▶

Now a jeep track (n.3) leads decidedly NW for a winding 200m ascent. A little after a *sorgente* (spring) is attractive **Rifugio al Montanaro** (1567m), self-catering, sleeps 12 – CAI members can request beds by phoning tel 0573 65074. Emergency room without beds always open.

Junction for paths leading off to Val d'Orsigna and Val Maresca.

Not far on is the four-way junction **Passo dei Malandrini** (1577m, **40min**), 'pass of evildoers', and the fork for Rifugio Porta Franca.

Detour via Rifugio Porta Franca
Fork R for the signed path high over a wild valley and on to solar-powered **Rifugio Porta Franca** (1580m, **40min**) ensconced in wood.

The last stretches climbing through woodland

Rifugio Porta Franca tel 0573 490338 (Info CAI Pistoia tel 0573 365582 or 335 207521), CAI, sleeps 40, open late July–Aug and weekends May–Oct. Great atmosphere if no mod cons, run with the help of volunteers who make sure you're fed well. Emergency room with fireplace always open. Drinking water outside.

As the name **'Porta Franca'** suggests, this spot on the border between erstwhile duchies and the papal state marks one of the points where duties levied on goods in transit were collected. A carriageway was even constructed here in the 1500s.

To rejoin the GEA, take the path behind the building diagonally up to the nearby crest to proceed N on a delightful level path accompanied by scented pinks, bilberries and wild orchids. A short way along is Fonte dell'Uccelliera (1686m) featuring a sizeable cross and a copious spring where n.00 is joined. Follow this to **Passo del Cancellino** to pick up the main route (**50min** from Rifugio Porta Franca).

After Passo dei Malandrini (1577m) the GEA/n.20 leads past the Surgente del Cacciatore (spring) to continue through the last pockets of beech cutting along the western flank of Poggio Malandrini. Then you finally emerge from tree cover to embark on a glorious alpine traverse NNW over the first of the many boundless carpets of bilberries and grass studded with gentians, pinks and lilies, and frequented by skylarks and birds of prey.

Nearby is pyramidal **Monte Gennaio** while ahead rears the huge barrier of dramatic bare ridges culminating in Corno alle Scale with its horizontal arenaceous stratifications (*scale* or 'steps') and summit cross; you can even see as far as the distant Libro Aperto, northwest and the Abetone pass, all to become familiar on Stage 15.

The delightful path heads up to join n.00 at **Passo del Cancellino** (1632m, **1hr**). You then need to mount a wide shoulder, steadily but not excessively steeply, to reach Passo dello Strofinatoio (1847m), opening into a beautiful glacially-formed pasture basin Piana della Calanchetta dotted with grazing sheep, its attractiveness marred somewhat by winter ski apparatus.

It is dominated by the abrupt point of Cupolino directly above the refuge building, while northwest is **Monte Spigolino**, formerly Fulgorino, as judicious shrines to Jove were erected on its summit in the hope that the god would direct his bolts of lightning there and save the towns!

Side trip to Corno alle Scale (30min return)
A must for anyone with time to spare, the Corno alle Scale enjoys brilliant views on a clear day. An easy path leads N to the broad 1945m uppermost crest of the sandstone block, and a chairlift. An invaluable orientation table tells you what you should be seeing: southwest to the Tyrrhenian Sea and islands, then north across the vast industrial Po plain to the Dolomites and numerous landmark alpine groups, such as glaciated Monte Rosa. Return the same way to Passo dello Strofinatoio.

From Passo dello Strofinatoio the final stretch for the day sticks to n.00 and the panoramic crest with a few more minor ups and downs, W for the most part. It transits by way of Passo dei Tre Termini (1785m), erstwhile border between Modena, Tuscany and the Papal State, then cruises over to **Lago Scaffaiolo** (1790m, **1hr 30min**) set in a slight depression on the crest dividing Tuscany from Emilia-Romagna.

Depending on conditions, **Lago Scaffaiolo** is either a sparkling blue lake or a shallow muddy pond. The name derives from 'caffa', an old term for a natural basin. The unassuming lake is the source of legends linked to the winds of amazing strength that come driving in unannounced from the west, gusting to the tune of 120kmph. Locals used to claim that even a pebble cast into the waters would stir up thick mist and unleash mighty storms, a belief immortalised by 14th-century writer Giovanni Boccaccio. Moreover it was long held that the lake was linked to the sea by a hidden channel.

Apart from the hopefully good views, another excellent reason to come is hospitable Rifugio Lago Scaffaiolo/ Duca degli Abruzzi, tel 0534 53390 or 347 7129414 **www.rifugiolagoscaffaiolo.it**, CAI, sleeps 28, open mid-June–mid-Sept and weekends except Nov. Named after a great explorer and mountaineer, it offers hot showers and pasta or polenta smothered with rich ragù. An earlier hut occupies the far side of the lake, successor of the earliest Italian Alpine Club refuge in the Apennines, dating back to 1878. It now serves as the refuge's emergency premises – always open with beds for six.

Exit route
Take the lane downhill NW then rough road to bar/restaurant **Rifugio Cavone** (1424m, **45min**) for the summer Tper bus to Porretta Terme for ongoing rail services.

The GEA leaves the trees at last and heads for Passo del Cancellino

STAGE 15
Lago Scaffaiolo to Boscolungo

Start	Lago Scaffaiolo
Distance	16km
Total ascent	500m
Total descent	900m
Grade	2–3
Time	6hr
Note	Short exposed stretches on the central section. A warning, echoed by the refuge staff: do not set out on this leg in unsettled weather or if thunderstorms are forecast. An alternative is to proceed via Passo Calanca for the Doganaccia–Cutigliano cable car then bus to Abetone.

An exhilarating – if tiring – walk that meticulously follows an elevated alpine-style ridge, a rocky tightrope with razor-thin profile, non-stop views and an amazing display of wildflowers along the way. It takes in a string of peaks before dropping through a magnificent state forest. Short exposed stretches on the central section necessitate a sure foot and are unsuitable for sufferers of vertigo.

The day's destination is the well-run friendly hostel at Boscolungo that does cheap sleeps and eats. Alternatively, if you want hotel accommodation and shops at the historic mountain resort of Abetone take the direct route from La Verginetta. From there it's only a 10min walk down the road to the start of Stage 16.

This is another ancient pass, once known as Colle dell'Ancisa, a reference to the practice of cutting tree trunks with a view to toppling them onto invading Romans.

Leave Lago Scaffaiolo on n.00 striking out NW along the ridge to Passo Calanca. ◄

Unless you need the exit path (WNW on n.66 for the Doganaccia cable car – **1hr**), take the middle path on a level around **Monte Spigolino** and towards a cluster of aerials. Just metres below them is a World War II memorial with guns and **Passo Croce Arcana** (1670m, **1hr**), 'arcane cross'.

This has been a **strategic pass** between the Po plain and the Tuscan coast for centuries, notably during the time of the Lombard Kingdom (6–8th century AD). In 1479 it witnessed the passage of 2000 horses and 500 foot soldiers belonging to a Milanese army, and was even paved in 1633.

At Passo Croce Arcana

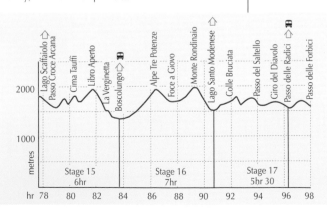

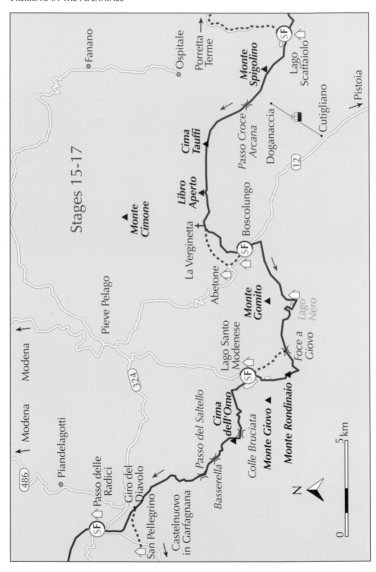

Stages 15-17

Fanano

Ospitale

Porretta Terme

Monte Spigolino

Lago Scaffaiolo

SF

Pistoia

Cima Tauffi

Passo Croce Arcana

Doganaccia

Cutigliano

12

Libro Aperto

Monte Cimone

La Verginetta

Boscolungo

SF

Abetone

Monte Gomito

Lago Nero

Pieve Pelago

Lago Santo Modenese

SF

Foce a Giovo

Modena

Modena

324

Cima dell'Omo

Passo del Saltello

Colle Bruciata

Monte Giovo

Monte Rondinaio

N

5 km

0

486

Piandelagotti

Passo delle Radici

Giro del Diavolo

Basserella

Castelnuovo in Garfagnana

San Pellegrino

SF

Head straight across the dirt road to climb the next knoll on the roller-coaster n.00 route, with historic stone markers. You'll find yourself in the company of gorgeous gentians, curious pink bistort and melodious skylarks, while shy marmots shelter in the valleys a short way below.

The next recognisable landmark is Colle dell'Acqua Marcia (1632m, where an exit path forks E, destination Ospitale). An uphill slog leads to **Cima Tauffi** (1799m), whose rocky top falls away dramatically with a near-vertical descent on loose shale terrain reminiscent of the English Lake District. The path negotiates an exposed shoulder and is known by local jokers as the *salto della morte*, the 'death leap'!

A string of narrow bare crests comes next – watch your step. A sequence of minor path junctions are encountered

Almost there: the final push to Libro Aperto

at broader grassbound saddles spread with bilberry shrubs, each a chance to bail out to lower altitudes before the stiff climb. Then due W a good path makes its way 300m upwards, with a final stretch NW for the top of **Libro Aperto** (1936m, **3hr**), also referred to as Monte Rotondo.

> The name **'open book'** can be better understood from the north as the arenaceous rock layers give the distinctive appearance of pages. This extremely rewarding scenic peak gives views to 2165m Monte Cimone due north, with its clutch of aerials, as well as Monte Rondinaio which is crossed on Stage 16.

Drop SW to a saddle and a vantage point with bird's-eye views of the Abetone resort and forest, continuing down across thick undulating carpets of bilberry and alpenrose. At last the descent begins in earnest, due W across grassland to the shelter of trees then the modest shrine and path junction at **La Verginetta** (1503m, **1hr**).

Direct route to Abetone (50min)

At the Abetone road pass

From **La Verginetta** keep on to a path fork then follow faint path n.00 over Monte Maiore (1560m). Down at a

spring and track junction take the straightforward lane down past a hut used in winter for *sci da fondo* (cross-country skiing). It's not far to the main road where you turn L for **Abetone** (1388m, **1hr**). Excellent value Hotel Regina (tel 057360007 www.albergoregina.com, accepts credit cards), shops, ATM, Copit buses to Pistoia and Modena.

> Abetone means 'big fir tree' in memory of a colossal exemplar felled to make way for the historic **Giardini–Ximenes road**; such was its girth that the outstretched arms of six men were insufficient to circle it completely! Huge twin pyramidal monuments commemorate the road's inauguration; it took from 1766 to 1778 to build at a cost of over two million lire to Tuscany, and over six million lire to Modena. Abetone is a renowned winter resort where skiing has been practised since 1904.

Only minutes along from La Verginetta, the GEA forks L on n.80, a jeep track with vestiges of old paving. It plunges SW into the depths of a magnificent forest of firs cared for by the Forestry Commission, home to nine different species of bats as well as huge numbers of industrious red wood ants. Down at a small cemetery a lane breaks off L, soon emerging on the road, virtually opposite the huge sign at the entrance for the hostel at **Boscolungo** (1337m, **1hr**).

> Ostello per la Gioventù tel 0573 60117 **www. ostelloabetone.it**, sleeps 100, open year-round. A short distance up the road is Hotel Primula (tel 0573 60108 **www.hotelprimula.com**, seasonal opening). Copit buses to Abetone, Pistoia and Modena.

STAGE 16

*Boscolungo to
Lago Santo Modenese*

Start	Boscolungo
Distance	15.5km
Total ascent	1060m
Total descent	900m
Grade	2–3
Time	7hr
Note	Towards the end of this stage is the climb to the summit of Monte Rondinaio (Grade 3 due to exposure); an easier variant with a saving of 1hr 40min is given from Foce a Giovo.

A really lovely day's walk that takes in more inspiring forest, pretty high-altitude lakes, long open scenic ridges and a memorable summit in a pure alpine ambience. It concludes at a renowned lake that despite its popularity has lost none of its charm, and has comfortable guesthouses offering a great overnight stay.

For route map and profile see Stage 15.

◀ From Boscolungo (1337m) the road alongside the Ostello quickly enters magnificent forest as a path, with red-spot waymarks at first. A broad forestry track is soon joined L, climbing gently SSE through an inspiring canopy of beech and silver fir.

After a ski piste, veer R (W) on n.102, an old mule track coasting through a beautiful side valley of beech and vivid laburnums, with the sound of running water far below. Sheer rock outcrops (*palestra di roccia*) are tackled by climbers, while circular clearings denote former use by charcoal burners. The way steepens with thinning woodland and open spaces crammed with purple orchids. Nearing the valley head, turn R off the lane

Lago Nero and the bivouac hut

for a well-marked path (n.104). This soon bursts onto grassland, a dense carpet of bilberry and juniper where you go R on n.100. A low rise is all that separates you from a cirque **Lago Nero** (1730m, **2hr**) set amid glacially smoothed rocks in sight of **Monte Gomito**, appropriately named for its sharp elbow shape. Close by is Bivacco Lagonero (property of CAI Pistoia, tel 329 3937299 for info).

Path n.100 continues high above the lake heading N through masses of wildflowers to Passo della Vecchia (1782m) overlooking Val di Luce with its ski infrastructures. Fork sharp L uphill for n.00; then at a ski piste veer L for the steady climb to the broad main ridge leading to the flowered expanse of Alpe Tre Potenze (1935m), a ski lift and a simply superb 360° outlook that takes in Corno alle Scale and Libro Aperto. The clear path moves on to Monte Femminamorta (1878m) then W in gentle descent, finally reaching **Foce a Giovo** (1674m, **2hr**), a saddle featuring a shrine.

Arriving at the saddle of Foce a Giovo

The jeep track here is the successor of the **politically motivated road** put through in the early 19th century to link the influential cities of Lucca to the south and Modena to the north, and pointedly detour their powerful rival, Florence. The story goes that the Duchess of Lucca and the Duke of Modena – who were betrothed – came face to face for the very first time halfway along the road. On seeing the advanced state and greying hair of her husband-to-be, the Duchess reportedly commented, 'It's snowing in the mountains,' to which he promptly responded, 'If it's snowing in the mountains then the cows should go back down to the valley.' The nuptials were called off...

Though it's a pity to miss the scenic stretches and aerial views of lakes, to avoid the moderately exposed climb to Monte Rondinaio, take the easy variant.

Easy route to Lago Santo Modenese (1hr 20min)

From **Foce a Giovo** straightforward path n.519 plunges downhill R (NW) past a curious stone pyramid and into woodland. Following the base of an immense rock ridge, it crosses patches of undulating grassy terrain passing a

waterfall that disappears over a cliff edge. It joins forces with the main route a short way below Lago Baccio for the final 10min to **Lago Santo Modenese**.

Cosy Rifugio Giovo on the banks of Lago Santo Modenese

For the main route, path n.00 effects a series of gentle ups and downs moving up to the main ridge, high above a string of lakes nestling below an imposing bastion topped with a cross, emanating from Monte Rondinaio. After a path junction a nick-like pass is reached, where the climb starts to become arduous. Exposed and steep but with brilliant views, it scrambles up the southeast shoulder, bright with purple asters, finally gaining superbly panoramic **Monte Rondinaio** (1964m, **1hr 30min**).

> The **second-highest point** on the whole of the trek (after Monte Prado) with views that take in the marvellous spread of the Garfagnana valley and the backdrop of the Alpi Apuane. True to its name, the Rondinaio summit swarms with zooming swallows, while the bare lower slopes are home to marmots. Beware of lingering late up here, however, as stories circulate of witches' gatherings and scary ghosts appearing in swirling mist...

It's all downhill from here so head via the easy rocky crest for 15min to a minor saddle, Valico del Passetto (1903m), former passage for the *via dei remi*, 'way of the oars'. ◄

Trunks from the Abetone forest were hauled this way en route to the Tyrrhenian coast for shipbuilding.

At this point you leave n.00 for n.523 down R. Thick juniper shrub cover precedes the welcome shade of beech woodland for the steady drop to lovely Lago Baccio (1554m), which boasts rushes, fish and picnic spots. At the far end of the lake, a well-trodden path drops through a beautiful wood past the junction for the easy variant. A short cut soon breaks off L to **Lago Santo Modenese** (1501m, **1hr 30min**).

Out of sight until the last minute, this **enchanting lake** nestles at the dramatic foot of Monte Giovo. At the most 20m deep, it abounds in trout and is a popular destination on weekends. The lake's 'santo' denomination may be attributable to the Latin 'sanctus' for 'unspoilt'. However, the locals are keen to perpetuate a Romeo-and-Juliet-like legend involving two young shepherds from opposite sides of the Apennine ridge, who belonged to families caught up in bitter disputes over logging rights. Once, utterly absorbed in each other, they failed to notice the lake's icy surface and were drowned in an eternal embrace. To this day a mysterious voice from the depths warns newcomers not to venture into the waters 'sanctified' by their love. Swim or paddle at your own risk...

Three friendly guesthouses are set tastefully around the tree-lined lakeside, accessible only on foot. You can expect to feast on trout, hearty pasta dishes and scrumptious desserts thick with luscious bilberries. Rifugio Vittoria tel 388 7412473 **www.rifugiovittoria.it**; Rifugio Marchetti tel 338 2909609; Rifugio Giovo tel 339 1676996 **www.rifugiogiovo.it**; all open May–Sept and weekends the rest of the year.

STAGE 17

Lago Santo Modenese to
Passo delle Radici

Start	Lago Santo Modenese
Distance	15.5km
Total ascent	670m
Total descent	645m
Grade	2
Time	5hr 30min
Note	The only difficulty may be encountered on the short, moderately exposed tract on the approach to Cime di Romecchio. A variant is given below.

A wonderful day's wandering with plenty of panoramic crests studded with wildflowers, and memorable views over the Garfagnana valley to the pale Alpi Apuane, renowned for providing Italian artists such as Michelangelo with top-grade marble for their masterpieces. You stay overnight in a well-run old-style hotel with a good restaurant. An exit is possible to the historic village of San Pellegrino.

▶ From Lago Santo Modenese at the rear of Rifugio Giovo path n.529 forks NW, moving high above the end

For route map and profile see Stage 15.

Approaching
Colle Bruciata

Near Cime di Romecchio the views range inland

The pass is a favourite with autumn hunters.

of the lake. Continue through the last of the beech woods past a spring and marshy saddle to a rise and Passo Boccaia (1582m). Branch L (due W) for the gentle climb across natural sandstone paving past a ruined shepherd's hut to incredibly scenic **Colle Bruciata** (1700m, **1hr 20min**), 'burnt col', also known as Passo Porticciola looking out to the sparkling distant Tyrrhenian, not to mention the Po plain northeast, Bismantova and Monte Prado. ◄

N.00 leads W cutting the flanks of rough **Cima dell'Omo**, popular with herds of inquisitive goats. You round a marvellously panoramic corner looking out to the Alpi Apuane. Not far along, just before trees are reached, turn R at a fork to coast back towards the main ridge. A bare slope of loose terrain is negotiated in ascent (take extra care in the wet), amid aromatic thyme and pinks. This superb scenic stretch proceeds just below the Cime di Romecchio.

A rough lane drops R to Sant'Anna on the Emilian side while L spells an exit to Barga in Tuscany.

A steep drop is followed by a level path between silver fir and beech to minor pass **Basserella** (1628m). ◄ Continue straight ahead on n.00 via a series of knolls marked with poles in and out of beech woodland to **Passo del Saltello**, also known as Bassa del Saltello (1599m, **2hr**), marked by a stone cross and dirt road. Now embark on the dirt track straight ahead through the muddy wood. At a bend 10min on, signed path n.00 breaks off R for a climb NNE to views of patch-work fields around Sant'Anna Pelago. Further on, hav-ing descended a little to the foot of a grass-ridden knoll (Monte Spicchio), the path widens into a pleasant track. An unsurfaced road is touched on (a feasible slightly shorter alternative which avoids the final ups and downs) but n.00 sticks tenaciously to the overgrown ridge. The two join up once and for all near the shrine at **Giro del Diavolo** (1659m, **1hr 30min**), the 'devil's circle'.

> As the legend goes, it was here that the devil did his utmost to lead **San Pellegrino** into temptation. Furious he had failed, he slapped the saint so hard that he twisted around in circles. Pilgrims walk up here carrying large stones that they deposit in the heap seen today, and turn around three times in recognition.

Exit route to San Pellegrino
At the marker column, take the easy path in steady descent through woodland bearing W to the slate roofs of **San Pellegrino** (1524m, **20min**).

> Home to a grand total of 15 permanent inhabitants, it is also the site of an ancient hospice. Purportedly founded by San Pellegrino, son of a Scottish king (whose embalmed body reposes in the church) it offered shelter to pilgrims and traders alike in the early Middle Ages.

> Café, shops, CCTNord bus to Castelnuovo in Garfagnana for trains. Hotel L'Appennino tel 0583 649069 **www.sanpellegrino.org**, accepts credit cards, open Easter–Nov, and L'Alpino tel 0583 649068.

From Giro del Diavolo with continuing glorious views, the GEA track heads along the ridge to Bocca dei Fornelli

The hotel at Passo delle Radici

(1630m), whence the road R (N) via Passo del Lagadello for the remaining 1.5km to **Passo delle Radici** (1527m, **40min**).

Old-style Hotel Lunardi tel 0583 649071 **www.albergolunardi.com** includes a recommended restaurant with generous meals, accepts credit cards. CTTNord bus to Castelnuovo in Garfagnana and trains.

STAGE 18

Passo delle Radici to
Passo di Pradarena

Start	Passo delle Radici
Distance	23km
Total ascent	1000m
Total descent	960m
Grade	2–3
Time	7hr 45min
Note	The Grade 3 stretch is encountered towards the end, between Le Porraie and Monte Sillano, where the path narrows across a steep mountainside, necessitating a sure foot – an easier variant is possible. The stage can be split into two more manageable sections (5hr/3hr 10min) by detouring off the ridge to Rifugio Bargetana.

A contender for the best stage on the GEA, this exhilarating (if tiring) haul takes in 2054m Monte Prado, the highest mountain in Tuscany and the loftiest point on the whole route. In the realms of the vast Parco Nazionale Appennino Tosco-Emiliano, the trek spends virtually all day on straightforward paths along wonderfully scenic grassy ridges ablaze with brilliant wildflowers in summer. At day's end a warm welcome and great food await, as well as comfortable rooms.

At Passo delle Radici (1527m) opposite the hotel take the lane N through a clearing with multi-coloured arrows denoting winter cross-country ski routes. Not far on is a green column marker where the GEA turns L up through shady beech woodland for the climb to the cleared top of Alpicella delle Radici (1678m). Keep on past a hut and follow red/white paint splashes for a faint route through the wood. A clearer path is soon joined up to a ridge popular with skylarks and gentians, leading via Cima La Nuda (1708m), a brilliant viewpoint to the mighty Alpi

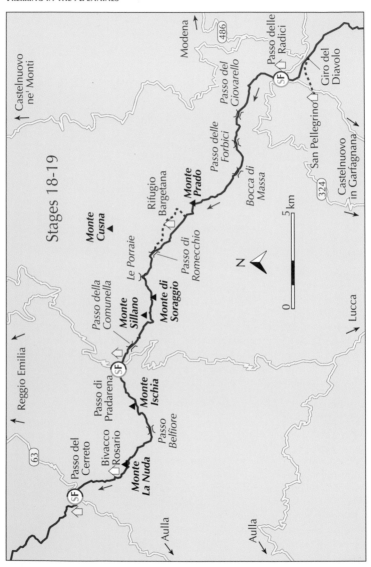

Stages 18-19

Castelnuovo ne' Monti →

← Reggio Emilia

Modena ↑

486

Passo delle Radici

SF

Giro del Diavolo

Passo del Giovarello

San Pellegrino

Castelnuovo in Garfagnana

324

Passo delle Forbici

Bocca di Massa

Monte Prado

Rifugio Bargetana

Monte Cusna

Passo di Romecchio

Le Porraie

Passo della Comunella

Monte Sillano

Monte di Soraggio

N

5 km

0

Lucca →

SF

Passo di Pradarena

Monte Ischia

Passo del Cerreto

63

Bivacco Rosario

Passo Belfiore

Monte La Nuda

SF

Aulla ↓

Aulla ↓

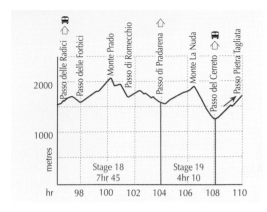

Apuane west and the Po plain in the opposite direction. It's a brief drop to **Passo del Giovarello** (1660m) and a metal cross.

Take the lane L (W) below Monte Giovarello down to **Passo delle Forbici** (1578m, **1hr 45min**).

Approaching Passo del Giovarello

The **'pass of the scissors'** features a tabernacle and commemorative plaque to a group of partisans – including a Russian – massacred in 1944 as World War II was drawing to a close. A 13th-century hospice once stood nearby, testifying to the passage of pilgrims.

Just around the bend take care not to miss the faint path R through a raspberry thicket and wood for a steady climb to bare crests with stunning views including Monte Prado northwest. Below is the Lama valley cloaked in dense forest and run through by watercourses. This glorious stretch touches on two 1800+m knolls and traverses a thick carpet of bilberries, purportedly the most extensive and productive in the whole of the Apennines!

Bocca di Massa (1800m) is a stony windswept pass with a column marker. Continue straight ahead NW to the iron cross and rock graffitti on Monte Cella (1942m). Next comes Passo degli Scaloni (1922m) followed by gentle

View from Monte Prado over the Lama valley

ascent guided by cairns to the summit of **Monte Prado** (2054m, **2hr 15min**) for 360° views. A brilliant spot!

Now it's NW down to broad saddle Sella di Monte Prado (1920m, **15min**) above Lago Bargetana. Here a detour and overnight stay at a friendly refuge is feasible.

Detour via Rifugio Bargetana

Leave the ridge route (R) on n.631. Not far after the lake is a lane which you follow L (NW) to family-run **Rifugio Bargetana** (1740m, **45min**), tel 328 2612737 www.rifugiobargetana.it, open June–Sept and weekends May and Oct, shower.

To rejoin the GEA take path n.633 in through woodland and bilberry thickets. With the odd up and down, you are led WNW to the ridge and **Passo di Romecchio** (1680m, **40min**).

The main GEA route continues over rocky terrain with cushions of tufted grass and marmot burrows.

Monte Cusna can be admired from La Focerella

North-northeast over Val d'Ozola is imposing Monte Cusna towering over a sea of trees. ◄

After Monte Castellino (1948m) comes a brief detour off the main ridge touching on La Focerella junction and rocky outcrop. The next important landmark is **Passo di Romecchio** (1680m, **1hr**) where the route from Rifugio Bargetana joins up.

Path n.00 proceeds past a shrine to San Bartolomeo and across apparently bare terrain. Tall grass occasionally obscures the way but red/white paint splashes recur at regular intervals. The next landmark is **Le Porraie** (1786m) pass. (Here n.639 drops R, a straightforward alternative but longer route to Passo di Pradarena.)

Keep L (W) high over a steep-sided pasture basin to cross the exposed rocky crest of **Monte di Soraggio**, helped by a short stretch of cable. While this is an exhilarating section, it is essential to watch your step. ◄ The path moves to the left (southern) side of the ridge to avoid climbing Monte Sillano. On easier terrain it hugs grassy slopes, dropping to beech wood. Don't miss the fork R (n.00) to a lane R (NW) leading over grassy hillsides with a radio mast. A couple of short cuts take you down to the broad saddle **Passo della Comunella** (1619m) before an imperceptible climb over Monte Asinara. As the pass and hotel come into view at the foot of Monte Cavalbianco, a signed path descends L past grazing horses to **Passo di Pradarena** (1575m, **2hr 30min**).

One of the earliest known passes in the Apennines, it dates back to the 3rd century AD due to the **Etruscan Via Clodia** that linked Parma with Lucca.

Modern-day visitors have the advantage of a tastefully decorated hotel with walkers' accommodation and innovative cuisine, Albergo Carpe Diem tel 0522 899151 www.albergocarpediem.com, open June–Oct and weekends the rest of the year, accepts credit cards.

STAGE 19

Passo di Pradarena to
Passo del Cerreto

Start	Passo di Pradarena
Distance	11.5km
Total ascent	510m
Total descent	830m
Grade	2–3
Time	4hr 10min

A superb walk with the highlight of the 1895m peak Monte La Nuda not to mention some amazing concentrations of wildflowers. A steep tiring descent brings you out at a well-served road pass.

▶ From Passo di Pradarena a clear lane moves off WSW through woodland on a level. A quarter of an hour later at an indistinct pass (Passo di Cavorsella), climb off L on n.00. In unrelenting ascent the trees are left behind and you are led out to rich meadows of mountain avens and fruit-loaded shrubs including juniper. After a saddle, the path bears L around the southern side of **Monte Ischia**, amid masses of cow parsley and daphne. After a brief drop through woodland is **Passo Belfiore** (1669m).

Continue in steady ascent past the Termine Tre Potenze, ('three powers' – a reference to historic boundaries), and curve NW passing just under the top of Cima Belfiore ('beautiful flower'). Below is the thickly wooded valley of the same name with roe deer grazing on the tree line, while screeching swifts will be overhead in summer.

Soon around the corner Monte La Nuda comes into view, recognisable for its rather unwieldy summit tower. The way narrows a little en route to a grassy neck near a rock obelisk, where marmots inhabit the slopes. You begin a climb through a jumble of fallen rocks on a clear

For route map and profile see Stage 18.

*The path approaching
Monte La Nuda*

Those lucky enough
to be here on a
clear day can expect
views north all the
way to the Alps.

path to a corrie where a fork L means the final winding
ascent via a minor fork, and to **Monte La Nuda** (1895m,
2hr 30min) and its derelict landmark tower. Marvellous
views range from the dramatic Valle dell'Inferno at your
feet with its Gendarme rock formation, and the ridges in
store on Stage 20. ◀

Backtrack briefly to the minor fork and faint marked
path R (W) over a narrow ridge to a saddle at the head of
Valle dell'Inferno with views over a lake and Passo del
Cerreto. Brace yourself for a steep knee-jerking plunge
R (NW) beneath chunky pinnacles, and watch your step
as the terrain can be slippery if wet. Down in a pasture
basin amidst a riot of buttercups, a flag points to the presence of cosy but basic **Bivacco Rosario** (1700m, **30min**),
where two people could just about squeeze in. Blankets
and firewood, water source nearby.

Path n.00 drops through woodland to where huge
jagged boulders sit amid broken trees – watch your step
here. Having reached holiday cabins you follow a lane
to the tarmac and go L. But the GEA soon takes a path

L parallel to the road and past a wind generator to **Passo del Cerreto** (1253m, **1hr 40min**).

Bivacco Rosario can only cater for limited numbers

> The pass was named for **Turkey oak**, probably at a time before forests were being cleared to make way for settlements. Centuries ago lumber from here was crafted into sledges for use in the marble quarries around Massa Carrara.

> Year-round ATN buses to Aulla for trains. Rooms and delicious meals at walker-friendly, family-run Hotel Passo del Cerreto (tel 0522 898214 or 0585 949666 **www.passodelcerreto.it**, accepts credit cards) or Albergo Ristorante Alpino tel 0522 714012 with run-down rooms but a good restaurant.

STAGE 20
Passo del Cerreto to
Prato Spilla

Start	Passo del Cerreto
Distance	16.5km
Total ascent	1130m
Total descent	1030m
Grade	2
Time	6hr 40min
Note	After Rifugio Città di Sarzano, the official GEA has been re-routed via Passo del Lagastrello. However, as this entails an excessively long 9hr haul to Lago Santo Parmense, here it has been organised as two stages with a detour to handy overnight stop at Prato Spilla, a small-scale ski resort with a comfortable hotel/restaurant. The direct route is also described below.

Apart from the initial bit, today the GEA momentarily abandons the main ridge (as it becomes a difficult scramble) and keeps to the eastern flank, passing through attractive wild valleys and a string of lakes in glacially formed landscapes. A series of tiring ups and downs is encountered, so be warned! Notwithstanding it's a great day, entering the Lunigiana region of Tuscany. Waymarks are unfortunately sorely lacking between Diga di Lagastrello and Prato Spilla.

Behind the eponymous hotel at Passo del Cerreto a well-worn path leads in and out of woodland, in common with a Sentiero Natura and its numbered poles. It coasts WNW easily towards Monte Alto, recognisable for its heavily eroded flanks. At a broad saddle you join a dirt track, keeping R, to nearby Passo dell'Ospedalaccio (1271m) named for a Benedictine pilgrim hospice that once stood here. ◀ Turn L on n.00 for an abrupt climb. Not far up, at a waymark column, it's R on n.671 across an erosion channel for a gentler traverse N below Monte

A curious marker bears the Napoleonic-era inscription 'Empire Français IX'.

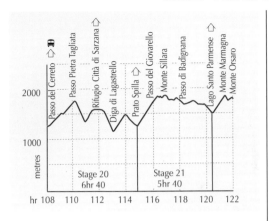

Alto. Yesterday's ridge and peaks are clearly visible, along with the northernmost outliers of the Alpi Apuane. A spring is passed then a minor pass gained.

The GEA heads towards Monte Alto

Here the route heads decidedly NW past charcoal burners' clearings into a pleasant side valley where the Torrente Secchia rises. The beautiful pasture basin **Prataccio** (1504m), crowned by slanting sandstone strata and home to multitudes of hawks, is traversed, and you veer L passing a fire-blackened boulder. Path n.671 zig-zags steeply NNW past clumps of Spanish broom to a notch in the rocky crest **Passo Pietra Tagliata** (1753m, **2hr**), 'cut stone pass'. To your left is the rugged crest Groppi di Camporaghena, while right the ridge keeps on for the Alpe di Succiso peak. And on a clear day you can even see all the way to the Alps!

Clear path n.673 winds down well-consolidated ancient moraine terraces into a partially wooded basin, little visited but for shy marmots. At the foot of immense rock slabs beneath Punta Buffanaro is the clearing and junction I Ghiaccioni (1375m). ◄ Proceed NW on path n.659. After crossing a stream, an inevitable steep ascent through shady beech woods leads to a fork (Costa del Lago, 1560m). Not long afterwards, the path coasts

An exit route goes N from here to the village of Succiso.

through trees and stony terrain past a small unnamed lake. A short distance on, at the base of the eponymous mount, is Lago di Monte Acuto, a tarn in a hanging valley. From the path signposts (unless you prefer to miss the hut), cross the lake outflow and follow the water's edge to where cosy timber cabin **Rifugio Città di Sarzana** (1580m, **1hr 40min**) nestles in the woods.

The view from Passo Pietra Tagliata back to Monte La Nuda

No mod cons such as hot water, but delicious dinners in atmospheric lamplight are a regular feature. Tel 339 2245117 **www.rifugiosarzana.it**, CAI, sleeps 25, open July–Aug and weekends. Emergency premises with 5 beds always open. The enthusiastic guardian lugs supplies up by rucksack.

Direct route via Passo del Lagastrello to Passo del Gioverello (4hr 30min)
Backtrack to the path signposts on the lakeside and take n.657 climbing W to Sella di Monte Acuto (1722m). After a short panoramic coast W, n.00 forks abruptly L (SW)

127

for a drop to Foce di Torsana (1322m). Monte Palerà is skirted to **Passo del Giogo** (1312m) then a road joined NNW for the last leg to **Passo Lagastrello** (1200m, **2hr**) and two renowned café-restaurants.

If needed the village of Comano is 12km away by road – slightly less if you branch S at Passo del Giogo. Accommodation at Hotel Miramonti (tel 0187 484563 **www.miramonti-albergo-ristorante.it**), ATN bus to Aulla and trains.

Follow the SP665 road downhill (Linari direction) to the first bend where n.00 breaks off R (W), not far above the ruins of a medieval abbey. After about 5mins, follow the GEA/n.110 sign to ascend the Torrente Taverone valley, through chestnut and beech. By climbing a spur, the open ridge is gained at **Foce Branciola** (1682m, **2hr**).

Now fork L (SW) on n.00 past old boundary stones to nearby **Monte Bocco** (1790m), a marvellous lookout. A stretch NW leads to **Passo del Gioverello** (1710m, **30min**), where the route from Prato Spilla is joined – see Stage 21.

Rifugio Città di Sarzana, a special hideaway in the woods

To proceed to Prato Spilla, pleasant path n.659 leaves the idyllic location of **Rifugio Città di Sarzana** in steady descent NW with lovely views. Ignore all turn-offs. Further down lies Lago Paduli and its dam **Diga di Lagastrello** (1153m, **1hr 15min**). Not far on at the roadside in Valle dei Cavalieri you cross a bridge L to the main road. ▸

Valle dei Cavalieri means 'valley of the knights', so-named from valorous events dating back to the Middle Ages.

Exit route to Rigoso (30min)
A turn R along this main road 2km away to the north is the village of Rigoso (1134m). Here you can take the TEP bus to Parma, or if you've missed it, stay at Camping Valdenza (café-restaurant, tent-less walkers can sleep in bungalows tel 0521 890300 or 331 3583889 www.campingvaldenza.it, open July–Aug then Fri–Sun April–June and Sept–Oct, groceries).

From the bridge turn L to the signposts announcing the Lunigiana region and start of path n.703, R uphill. Lago Squincio is passed, and thereafter the way heads W through woodland in a steady zigzagging climb via surprising numbers of charcoal burners' clearings. After **Passo Sasseda** (1479m) comes the inevitable plunge – but on a faint path so keep your eyes peeled for waymarks. A short way down is Lago Scuro, which dwindles to a damp patch most summers. At its far end a rough lane leads through to more substantial Lago Verdarolo (1388m), true to its greenish name.

Here n.703 drops across the lake mouth to veer L along the opposite shore to picnic tables where a lane with white and lime-green waymarks is joined. This leads NW, narrowing to a clear path where red/white markings reappear. After a lovely lookout is an unsurfaced road. A matter of metres uphill L is **Prato Spilla** (1351m, **1hr 45min**). Though modest in alpine terms, this is an important ski resort for the Apennines. Thankfully it also has a comfortable Albergo Prato Spilla (tel 0521 890194 or 331 9481820 www.pratospilla.pr.it, open year-round, accepts credit cards) with helpful, friendly staff and creative dinners.

STAGE 21
*Prato Spilla to
Lago Santo Parmense*

Start	Prato Spilla
Distance	13.5km
Total ascent	790m
Total descent	630m
Grade	2–3
Time	5hr 40min
Note	Keep off this ridge route in high winds or bad weather. There's a short moderately exposed stretch prior to Monte Brusa in the latter part.

Arguably the best stage of the whole GEA, today's trek ambles along superbly magnificent panoramic crests. It touches on so many delightful lakes set in glacially moulded hanging valleys that you lose count! No wonder the National Park here used to be known as 'cento laghi' (100 lakes). There are good chances too of sighting the many birds of prey that frequent the high open uplands. The day's conclusion is a divine turquoise tarn with a memorable refuge set on its bank amid beautiful forest.

For route map and profile see Stage 20.

◄ Uphill from the hotel entrance at Prato Spilla is the start of n.705 (not waymarked at first), a rough track that follows the grassy ski slope uphill SSW. Keep to the right side to avoid the steeper bits. Around 20min on, it veers R (red/white markers) continuing uphill as a lane, R again under a ski lift. Now a path, it crosses a couple of streams and traverses another ski piste. After a rise near marshy terrain colonised by cotton grass, look to your R for the sign for n.705. This regularly marked path climbs through woodland, emerging on soft cushiony upland near the rocky base of **Monte Torricella**, and a great lookout over Lago Verde, backed by shapely Monte Navert. Glacially modelled sandstone slabs and carpets of bilberries are crossed en route to minuscule Lago Martini

and a decisive turn L (S) for the brief climb to **Passo del Giovarello** (1710m, **1hr 15min**), an arduous pass dominating a wild precipitous valley. The views spread south to where the striking Alpi Apuane rise majestically over the Garfagnana valley.

The route up a ski piste above Prato Spilla

Route n.00 – and the official GEA – are rejoined as you move off NW to ascend the bare 1835m hump that goes by the name of Monte Bragalata. (The actual top can be detoured on the clear path that breaks off R skirting the mount and rejoining the main path prior to Passo Compione.)

Improving views take in the promising procession of ridges snaking ahead and the Pontremoli valley running inland from the Tyrrhenian coast. In the opposite direction, inland, lies the pretty Laghi di Compione then modest reliefs dwindling away to the flat Po plain.

An easy descent concludes at Passo Compione (1794m). Subsequently there's an amazingly scenic ridge

The beautiful Sillara lakes

The name, of ancient Ligurian origin, may refer to its near-vertical shape. An exhilarating spot, it sports clumps of thrift and a Madonna statue, and fascinating views.

Another name of ancient Ligurian origin, it is believed to signify 'heap of stones' and not 'crazy', as the Italian word would seem to imply.

stretch above the beautiful Laghi di Sillara occupying a broad shelf as the mountain slopes valleywards. A short but steep climb away is **Monte Sillara** (1859m, **1hr**). ◄

Across dry slopes colonised by noisy crickets and a colossal cairn, you pass below Monte Paitino (1817m) and some impressive rock needles. A slight drop leads to a path junction Sella di Paitino (1764m) where the beautiful twin Lagoni lakes can be admired, nestling in forest far below.

Now fork L (W) for the snaking, increasingly narrow path via ledges at times. Ignore turn-offs and stick to n.00 for the superbly panoramic rocky promontory of **Monte Matto** (1837m), marked by a cross. ◄ A surprisingly abrupt drop follows on a faint crest path to Passo di Badignana (1680m, **1hr 15min**).

Keep straight on amid rose bushes, high above the vast valley dominated by nearby Monte Scala. The inevitable climb follows as the path negotiates a narrow, moderately exposed crest edged by audacious beech trees that have crept up from the northern side, giving welcome patches of shade as the path dips into the wood. A broader grassy crest leads to the last noteworthy summit of the day, Monte Brusa (1796m), 'burnt mount', colonised by pretty houseleek plants.

The descent NW affords a good look at Lago Pradaccio at the foot of towering Rocca Biasca. Close at hand is **Passo delle Guadine** (1687m, **1hr**). Branch R (NNW) on n.719 across especially rewarding bilberry 'orchards' and down through woodland to Sella della Sterpara (1646m). A gentle drop through conifers passes two key GEA junctions (for Stage 22 and the short cut), but for now stick to n.719 (R) for the final 20min descent over sandstone slabs to the lake, which you don't get to

Rifugio Mariotti and lovely Lago Santo Parmense ringed by trees

see properly until you've all but fallen in the water as it is ringed by thick woodland. Superbly set on the western edge of **Lago Santo Parmense** (1508m, **1hr 10min**) is hospitable **Rifugio Mariotti**.

> Rifugio Mariotti tel: 0521 889334 or 349 2260668 **www.rifugiomariotti.it**, CAI, sleeps 42, open June–Sept and weekends; shower. Don't miss the scrumptious *tortelli con patate* (pasta parcels stuffed with potato). One of the earliest refuges in Italy, the historic building dates back to 1882.

> The **unbelievably blue lake**, home to two types of trout, has a surface area of 81,500 m² and is an astonishing 22.5m deep – a building seven storeys high would disappear in it, as the custodian delights in telling visitors. As is the case for Lago Santo Modenese, in all likelihood 'santo' derives from 'unspoilt' rather than a reference to a long-gone hermit or 'holy' man.

Exit route to Rifugio Lagdei and Bosco

A stroll away from the lakeside is a chairlift for the descent. Otherwise allow 30min for either of the signed paths dropping through woodland to the road and Rifugio Lagdei (1312m).

> Tel 0521 889353 or 333 2443053 **www.rifugiolagdei.it**, open all year. It's 6km down to the village of Bosco, which boasts family-run Albergo Ghirardini tel 0521 889123 **www.albergoghirardini.it**, groceries and TEP buses to Parma.

STAGE 22
Lago Santo Parmense to
Passo della Cisa

Start	Lago Santo Parmense
Distance	20km
Total ascent	870m
Total descent	1370m
Grade	2–3
Time	6hr 30min
Note	Inadvisable in inclement weather; the stage is long and tiring, so pace yourself carefully. A short cut is given at the start (saving 1hr 10min); however, it misses out the best belvedere summits.

This marvellous roller-coaster stage gets off to an amazing start with three spectacular peaks in rapid succession. It sticks faithfully with the main Apennine ridge enjoying awesome views that embrace the Tyrrhenian coast and Liguria, as well as the inland plain around Parma. Birds of prey patrol the sky and the terrain is mostly grassy, smothered with memorable wildflowers such as colourful lilies. In the second half of the stage waymarks are few and far between, and elevations lower as the GEA visits pasture grazed by cows and horses.

Lengthy stretches follow evocative paved mule tracks dating back to medieval times when they witnessed the passage of pilgrims and traders. One route, the Via del Sale, was set up to smuggle salt as it was heavily taxed. More recently wartime black marketeers trafficking in much-needed goods trod the same routes, as did partisans and escapees such as the author Eric Newby.

From Lago Santo Parmense retrace your steps on path n.719 along the wooded southwestern shore of the lake then in ascent to the junction (30min) where the GEA branches R (NW) on n.723. It climbs quickly out of the wood, passing curious rock piles and up to Sella Marmagna (1781m) with glorious views to the Tyrrhenian

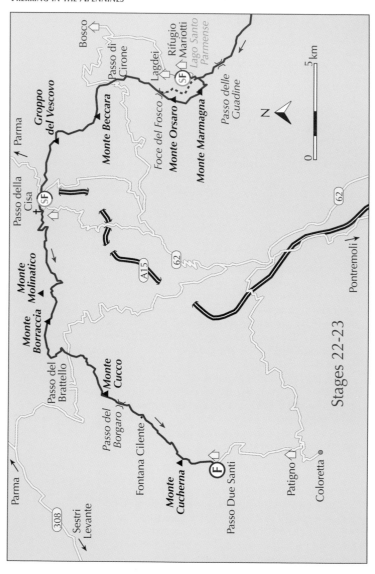

Bosco

Rifugio
Mariotti

Passo di
Cirone

Lagdei

Lago Santo
Parmense

*Groppo
del Vescovo*

SF

Parma

Monte Beccara

Foce del Fosco

Monte Orsaro

Passo delle
Guadine

Monte Marmagna

N

5 km

0

Passo della
Cisa

SF

62

*Monte
Molinatico*

A15

62

Pontremoli

*Monte
Borraccia*

Passo del
Brattello

*Monte
Cucco*

Passo del
Borgaro

Fontana Cilente

Stages 22-23

*Monte
Cucherna*

F

Patigno

Parma

Passo Due Santi

Coloretta

308

Sestri
Levante

Walkers enjoying the views on Monte Marmagna

The unusual denomination is a derivation of 'Markman' for Germanic 'border dwellers' who settled on its flanks when the Romans left the area.

coast. Turn R (not straight up) for an easy route to **Monte Marmagna** (1851m, **1hr**), complete with a 1901 iron cross, and fabulous 360° views. ▶

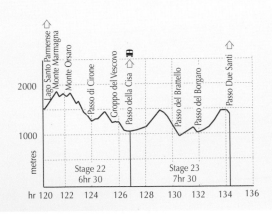

*Amazing stretch
en route to
Monte Braiola*

This ancient Lombard
name is a reference
to 'free pasture'.

Narrower now, n.00 drops NW around a tight corner amid impressive slanted rock strata and down to Sella della Braiola (1715m) followed by the inevitable puff up to Monte Braiola (1819m) from where the day's destination, Passo della Cisa, can be seen. ◄ A plunge ends at Bocchetta dell'Orsaro (1722m) where you need to brace yourself for the ensuing haul but first the n.00 ducks briefly L before veering R around an old landslip, to gain the rocky crest studded with houseleeks. The summit of **Monte Orsaro** (1830m, **1hr**) 'bear mount', hosts a slender sculpture looking out over the Magra river valley that runs inland from La Spezia.

On easier terrain you descend through bilberry shrubs on a rutted path into woodland to join an old mule track with stone edging and the short cut. Nearby L is the saddle **Foce del Fosco** (1613m, **30min**).

Short cut to Foce del Fosco (1hr 20min)
From **Lago Santo Parmense** (1508m), in common with the main route, retrace your steps along the lake edge

and uphill, but fork R for n.729 at the first key junction. This loops NW past a peat bog bright with marsh marigolds then downhill via glacially modelled slabs. On the edge of beech woods facing the lower southern slope of Monte Orsaro is a path junction at 1600m in sight of the hut Capanna del Braiola. Not far on, fork L on n.727a, a gentle climb on a pleasant broad mule track with stone embankments. This gains a wooded ridge and proceeds on a level to the foot of Monte Fosco and **Foce del Fosco** (1613m, **1hr 20min**) where it joins the main GEA route.

From Foce del Fosco the GEA quickly reaches lake look out Monte Fosco (1680m) and a lovely old stone pillar bearing the crown denoting the erstwhile border of the Duchy of Parma. Now comes a knee-testing descent to Bocchetta del Tavolo (1444m, **30min**).

Due N n.00 leads up a sunken lane and over a stile to a clearing thick with raspberries (ignore the fork for Monte Tavola as it is overgrown). Scenic meadows with grazing cows and coloured by meadow saffron and bistort are crossed. Then it's back to shady woodland teeming with squirrels, descending to a succession of grassy knolls. After a graceful Romanesque-style chapel, a recent construction that occupies the site of a historic hospice, a lane leads to nearby road pass **Passo di Cirone** (1265m, **40min**). ▶ About 1km to the R (E) along the road is a café-restaurant, a detour off the GEA.

Keep straight ahead, around the traffic barrier and onto a jeep track N lined with masses of purple bugloss. Only minutes on, with the restaurant roof visible, branch R on a path heading towards tree cover and waymarks. This drops a little beneath a crumbling outcrop, going L where it is joined by a lane which bears W along a fence.

Further on, immediately after a makeshift livestock gate, fork L on the faint path uphill over bare terrain to **Monte Beccara** (1379m) and another weather-worn border marker. The marvellous views will hopefully take in the Alps across the mugginess of the Po plain, in addition to the raised motorway above Pontremoli. From here on

Long known to smugglers, in the late 1800s the pass was used by skilled timber workers on their way to Corsica to make sleepers for the railway.

One of the old marker stones on the way to Passo della Cisa

the mountains are gentler and lower in altitude, the dramatic ridge and peaks left behind.

A slight dip is followed by more panoramic crest then a rutted track N through pasture in gradual descent in the company of yellow poles for the *metanodotto*, the underground gas pipeline. Keep straight through a conspicuous saddle. Not far up, the GEA leaves the lane to go L up wooden steps to gain the upper edge of the elongated **Groppo del Vescovo** (1243m, **1hr 40min**), the 'bishop's mount'. Descend the other side to a 1176m pass and lane junction; believe it or not, more ascent awaits!

Take care not to go straight up the other side this time, but keep slightly L of the main crest (still n.00) cutting through trees and boar diggings up to the top. Enjoying wide-ranging views it heads to a pylon on Monte Valoria (1229m) and masses of gorgeous thistles. At a shrine with dizzy views over the autostrada, you finally begin to descend gently W into mixed woodland of hazel and oak, in common with the Via Francigena. A broad lane takes over further on and you coast easily into **Passo della Cisa** (1041m, **1hr 10min**).

The name comes from the Latin for 'cut' as the Romans put a road through here. Modern engineers have excavated one of the most important **Apennine motorway tunnels** kilometres underground, though you wouldn't know it.

Snack bars, restaurants, groceries, souvenirs galore. The TEP Prontobus service can be used as far as Berceto and trains. For accommodation: 20min/1.5km L (S) down the road Locanda degli Aceri tel 0187 836421 locandadegli-aceri@lunigiana.net offers good-value rooms and a restaurant that serves flavoursome *testaroli al pesto*, pasta squares served with fragrant basil sauce, a clear sign that you're on the doorstep of Liguria. In the opposite direction from Passo della Cisa, 2km away is a walkers' hostel tel 0525 629072 or 328 8741814 www.ostellipassocisa.it, sleeps 24, open April–Sept; can be unreliable.

STAGE 23

*Passo della Cisa to
Passo Due Santi*

Start	Passo della Cisa
Distance	25km
Total ascent	1070m
Total descent	600m
Grade	2
Time	7hr 30min
Note	Waymarking on the last section is not especially frequent so keep your eyes peeled at the main junctions and don't continue too far without checking for red/white paint splashes.

This concluding stage to the marvellous GEA entails problem-free walking mostly on wide forestry tracks and lanes. Woodland dominates, but there are plenty of open tracts with inspiring views. Halfway is Passo del Bratello with a handy café/restaurant and exit route if needed. Food and accommodation is available at the pass at the trek end, but a more suitable place to celebrate is the tiny village of Patigno, 5km downhill.

For route map and profile see Stage 22.

◀ From Passo della Cisa, in common with a brief stretch of the via Francigena, head up steps past the grey stone church dedicated to Nostra Signora della Guardia, built in 1921 on a former customs post. Keep L (W) on the lane along the crest into shady woodland; you soon part ways with the VF and keep to n.00 in steady ascent. A fork L sees you pass a forestry hut and picnic table on a stony path. Not far up the GEA/n.00 veers sharp L (SSE) as a path up to a wooded ridge. At the top it heads R (W) on a level stretch through beechwood, occasional openings affording glimpses of the coast. A spring is touched on before a brief loop S. Further on in a clearing, the GEA leaves the wood to turn R on a rutted track. This heads towards a communications tower on **Monte Molinatico**, but without actually reaching it as you fork L at a signed junction (1460m, **2hr 10min**). A broad lane now leads NW in easy descent via 1329m Monte Ferdana then 1259m **Monte Borraccia** with brilliant views over the Magra river valley and back to the silhouetted Alpi Apuane.

After a hut and over a rise close to Monte Croce di Ferro, red/white markers on a rock point you L down to a second lane fork where it's L again (SW) in hazel and oak wood, to emerge at the road and **Passo del Brattello** (948m, **1hr 30min**), café-restaurant and a memorial to

Open rocky terrain after Passo del Borgaro

partisans executed during World War II. Bratto, 2km away L (E) has an ATN bus for Pontremoli.

Straight across the road follow the lane past a chapel and pylons and into the cool shade of the Foresta del Brattello, home to thousands of Christmas trees. Stick with the lane mostly SW touching on huts and a series of picnic areas beneath conifers. Yellow poles of a buried *metanodotto* (gas pipeline) are followed past a traffic barrier; watch out for red/white markers on the tree trunks at the many junctions. **Monte Cucco** (1128m) is traversed, though due to the dense forest you wouldn't know it, and not far ahead via rock slabs is **Passo del Borgaro** (1013m, **1hr 15min**), recognisable for its pylon and extensive panorama all the way back to Monte Orsaro.

Here the GEA/n.00 forks R for a narrow path through tall bracken and woodland of chestnut and juniper. A marvellously open crest, brilliant with masses of Mediterranean aromatic herbs and hardy flowering plants, gives views inland over the Taro valley and tiny settlements nestling in woodland. At a monument to

A monument to World War II partisans overlooks the Taro valley

World War II partisans, join a lane. At the ensuing intersection keep R to Fontana Cilente, a deliciously cool spring. A path uphill under a power line rejoins a lane amid a concentration of silver birch for steady ascent, before levelling out over sandy terrain. A clearing with hunters' structures is traversed, then a stony rough way continues to the 1470m mark on the western flank of Monte Cucherna. Mostly S on a wide lane that can get muddy, it finally reaches **Passo Due Santi** (1385m, **2hr 35min**) on the border between Tuscany and Emilia Romagna; half of a chapel there stands in one region, half in the other. You made it!

Café, restaurant. Accommodation at Zum Zeri/Al Cinghiale Bianco tel 328 2893612 or 0187 1855401 **www.ilcinghialebianco.it**, Aug–Oct.

Better still, stay down the hill at the pretty village of Patigno (750m, 5km away) with old stone houses shaded by scented lime trees and frequented by screeching swifts. Accommodation providers will pick up walkers from Passo Due Santi: arrange this when booking.

Family-run hotel-restaurant La Catinella tel 0187 447125 or 339 8266704 albergolacatinella@libero.it. Cafés, groceries, ATN buses to Pontremoli, 17km away. Further down the road at Noce (2km) is the converted mill Agriturismo Mulino Marghen tel 339 8456395 **www.mulinomarghen.com**.

Pontremoli in the Magra river valley boasts a graceful medieval bridge, an important museum with prehistoric anthropomorphic stele statues dating back to 3000BC. Shops, hotels, ATM, Tourist Info and excellent train links to Bologna and Florence.

A wonderful follow-up to the GEA is to head for La Spezia and spend time lazing on the famous spectacular Cinque Terre coast, or taking the dizzy pathways along the breathtaking terraces.

APPENDIX A
Route summary table

Stage	Start/Finish	Time	Distance	Ascent/Descent	Grade	Page
1	Bocca Trabaria/Passo di Viamaggio	6hr 45min	19km	750m/820m	2	44
2	Passo di Viamaggio/Caprese Michelangelo	5hr 10min	17.5km	500m/850m	2	49
3	Caprese Michelangelo/La Verna	5hr 45min	17km	1030m/560m	1–2	52
4	La Verna/Badia Prataglia	7hr	23.5km	575m/870m	2	56
5	Badia Prataglia/Rifugio Città di Forlì	6hr 10min	18.5km	1040m/430m	1–2	60
6	Rifugio Città di Forlì/Passo del Muraglione	4hr 30min	13.5km	470m/920m	2	64
7	Passo del Muraglione/Colla di Casaglia	6hr 20min	23km	700m/700m	2	69
8	Colla di Casaglia/Badia Moscheta	5hr 45min	19.25km	450m/800m	1–2	73
9	Badia Moscheta/Passo del Giogo	2hr 10min	8km	300m/0m	1–2	78
10	Passo del Giogo/Passo della Futa	5hr 15min	13.5km	600m/580m	2–3	80
11	Passo della Futa/Montepiano	4hr 30min	14.5km	420m/620m	2	84
12	Montepiano/Rifugio Pacini	5hr 15min	17km	850m/550m	2	87
13	Rifugio Pacini/Pracchia	6hr 50min	24.2km	600m/960m	2	91
14	Pracchia/Lago Scaffaiolo	6hr 20min	16km	1450m/300m	2–3	94
15	Lago Scaffaiolo/Boscolungo	6hr	16km	500m/900m	2–3	100
16	Boscolungo/Lago Santo Modenese	7hr	15.5km	1060m/900m	2–3	106

Stage	Start/Finish	Time	Distance	Ascent/Descent	Grade	Page
17	Lago Santo Modenese/Passo delle Radici	5hr 30min	15.5km	670m/645m	2	111
18	Passo delle Radici/Passo di Pradàrena	7hr 45min	23km	1000m/960m	2–3	115
19	Passo di Pradàrena/Passo del Cerreto	4hr 10min	11.5km	510m/830m	2–3	121
20	Passo del Cerreto/Prato Spilla	6hr 40min	16.5km	1130m/1030m	2	124
21	Prato Spilla/Lago Santo Parmense	5hr 40min	13.5km	790m/630m	2–3	130
22	Lago Santo Parmense/Passo della Cisa	6hr 30min	20km	870m/1370m	2–3	135
23	Passo della Cisa/Passo Due Santi	7hr 30min	25km	1070m/600m	2	142

APPENDIX B
Italian–English glossary

abbazia	abbey
acqua non controllata	water not analysed for drinking
acqua (non) potabile	water (not) suitable for drinking
addestramento cani da caccia	training ground for hunting dogs
affittacamere	rooms to rent
agriturismo	farm with meals and/or accommodation
albergo	hotel
alimentari	grocery shop
alloggio	accommodation
alto	high, upper
aperto	open
area attrezzata	picnic area
autostazione	bus, coach station
autostrada	toll-paying motorway
badia	abbey
basso	low, lower
bestiame al pascolo	grazing livestock
biglietto	ticket
biglietteria	ticket office
bivio	path fork
bocca	pass, literally 'mouth'
bosco	wood
caccia	hunting
camera, stanza	room
campeggio permesso/vietato	camping allowed/forbidden
capanna	hut
carta escursionistica	walking map
castello	castle
centro visita	visitors' centre
chiesa	church
chiudere il cancello	close the gate
chiuso	closed
colle, colla	pass
collina	hill
crinale	main ridge
croce	cross, crucifix

diga	dam
divieto di accesso/caccia/campeggio	entry/hunting/camping forbidden
enoteca	wine bar, shop
entrata	entry
eremo	monastic retreat, hermitage
fermata di autobus	bus stop
fiume	river
fonte, sorgente	spring, fountain
foresta demaniale	state forest
foresteria	hostel-style accommodation
frana	landslide
frazione	hamlet
funivia	cable-car
giogo	pass, literally 'yoke'
groppo	knoll
grotta	cave
innesto	link
lago	lake
maneggio	horse-riding
maestà	wayside shrine, tabernacle
metanodotto	gas pipeline
montagna, monte	mountain
mulattiera	mule track
museo	museum
ostello	hostel
osteria	tavern
palestra di roccia	rock-climbing wall
panificio	bakery
pericolo/pericoloso	danger/dangerous
pieve	village
poggio	hill, knoll
ponte	bridge
Posto Tappa	walker's accommodation
prato	meadow
proprietà privata	private property
ricovero invernale	refuge winter premises
rifugio	mountain refuge
santuario	sanctuary, hermitage
sbocco	pass
seggiovia	chairlift

segheria	sawmill
segnaletica	waymarking
sella	saddle
sentiero	path
sentiero attrezzato	aided path (with fixed cables)
sentiero natura	nature trail
stazione ferroviaria	railway station
strada	road
strada forestale	forestry track
strada sterrata	unsealed road
supermercato	supermarket
tabernacolo	tabernacle, shrine
torrente	stream
trattoria	restaurant
uscita	exit
uso cucina	kitchen facilities
valico	pass
viottolo	country lane
vipera	viper, adder

Handy bus/train terminology

biglietto di andata (andata-ritorno)	single (return) ticket
cambio a...	change at...
coincidenza	connection
feriale	working days ie Mon–Sat
festivo	Sun and public holidays
giornaliero	daily
sciopero	strike
scolastico	school days
soppresso	no service
da...a...	from...to...(dates)

Useful expressions

Good morning	*Buongiorno*
Good evening	*Buona sera*
Goodnight	*Buona notte*
Good-bye and thank you	*Arrivederci e grazie*
Do you speak English?	*Parla inglese?*
On the phone: Hello, I'd like a single/doubleroom for tomorrow night	*Pronto, vorrei una camera singola/dop pia per domanisera*

How much is it?	*Quanto costa?*
Do you take credit cards?	*Posso pagare con la carta dicredito?*
Is breakfast/dinner included?	*E' inclusa la colazione/cena?*
What time is breakfast/dinner?	*A che ora è la colazione/cena?*
I'm vegetarian/vegan/coeliac	*Sono vegetariano/vegano/celiaco*
What's on today?	*Che cosa c'è oggi?*
Can I pitch my tent here?	*Posso montare la mia tenda qui?*

APPENDIX C
Useful contacts

Local transport

Trains
Trenitalia
tel 892021
The Italian State railway network
www.trenitalia.com

FCU
tel 075 9637637
www.umbriamobilita.it
For the Roma–Sansepolcro railway

TFT
tel 800 922984
www.trasportoferroviariotoscano.it
Branch line from Arezzo via Bibbiena
to Stia

Buses
AMV
tel 800 373760
www.amvbus.it
Passo del Muraglione–San Godenzo,
Colla di Casaglia, Passo del Giogo,
Passo della Futa

ATN
Autolinee Toscana Nord
tel 800 223010
www.atnsrl.it
Passo del Cerreto, Passo del Brattello,
Bratto, Patigna, Pontremoli

Baschetti
tel 0575 749816
www.baschetti.it
Sansepolcro–Bocca Trabaria–Urbino–
Pesaro run, Mon–Fri only

CAP
www.capautolinee.it
Montepiano, Passo della Collina

CTTNord
tel 800 570530
www.lucca.cttnord.it
Castelnuovo di Garfagnana–Passo delle
Radici and San Pellegrino

Copit
tel 848 800730
www.copitspa.it
Boscolungo, Abetone

Etruria Mobilità
tel 800 922984
www.etruriamobilita.it
Arezzo, Sansepolcro, Passo di
Viamaggio, Pieve Santo Stefano,
Caprese Michelangelo, Fragaiolo,
Chiusi La Verna, Badia Prataglia,
Camaldoli

Prontobus
tel 840 222223
Phone one one day ahead to book a minibus
link Passo della Cisa via Berceto to the
train line at the cost of a normal fare

Sansepolcro Taxi
tel 335 5234282 or 347 4962625
www.sansepolcrotaxi.it

StartRomagna
www.startromagna.it
Campigna, Forlì

TEP
tel 840 222222
www.tep.pr.it
Rigoso, Parma

Tper
www.tper.it
Porretta Terme, Rifugio Cavone

Tourist information
The region traversed by the GEA is peppered with towns and helpful information offices. The most useful are:
Abetone
tel 0573 60231
www.pistoia.turismo.toscana.it

Arezzo
tel 0575 401945
www.arezzointuscany.it

Bibbiena
tel 0575 593098

Bologna
tel 051 239660
www.bolognawelcome.com

Borgo San Lorenzo
tel 055 8456230

Castelnuovo di Garfagnana
tel 0583 641007
www.castelnuovogarfagnana.org

La Spezia
tel 0187 770900
www.turismoprovincia.laspezia.it

Parma
tel 0521 218889
www.turismo.comune.parma.it

Pieve Pelago
tel 0536 71304
www.pievepelago.info

Pistoia
tel 0573 374401
www.turismo.pistoia.it

Pontremoli
tel 0187 832000
www.aptmassacarrara.it

Porretta Terme
tel 0534 22021
www.comune.porrettaterme.bo.it

Prato
tel 0574 24112
www.pratoturismo.it

Reggio Emilia
tel 0522 451152
http://turismo.comune.re.it

Sansepolcro
tel 0575 740536
www.valtiberinaintoscana.it

Maps
Online bookshop in Florence, Italy
www.stella-alpina.com

Stanfords (London and Bristol, UK)
www.stanfords.co.uk

The Map Shop (Upton upon Severn, Worcestershire, UK)
www.themapshop.co.uk

Other sources of information
Austrian Alpine Club in the UK
http://aacuk.org.uk

Club Alpino Italiano
www.cai.it

www.lineagotica.eu
For information about the World War II Gothic Line

Parco Nazionale delle Foreste Casentinesi
www.parcoforestecasentinesi.it

Parco Nazionale dell'Appennino Tosco-Emiliano
www.parcoappennino.it

APPENDIX D
Background reading

JW von Goethe's *Italian Journey: The Collected Works, volume 6* (Princeton University Press, 1989), makes several inspired mentions of the Apennines. Eric Newby's moving account of his wartime experience *Love and War in the Apennines* (Picador, 1983) paints a fascinating picture of village life as well as rendering homage to the courageous Italians who risked their lives to help escaping Allied PoWs following the 1943 Armistice. Nowadays, as an ongoing way of saying 'thank you', the Monte San Martino Trust www.msmtrust.org.uk offers young Italians bursaries to study English in the UK, while the Escape Lines Memorial Society organises annual treks, keeping in touch with the villages www. ww2escapelines.co.uk.

Wildflower enthusiasts will appreciate the handy Cicerone pocket guide *Alpine Flowers* by Gillian Price (2014), as well as Christopher Grey-Wilson and Marjorie Blamey's *Alpine Flowers of Britain and Europe* (HarperCollins, 1995) alas long out of print though available second hand. Birdwatchers need go no further than Bruun, Delin and Svensson's excellent *Birds of Britain and Europe* (Hamlyn, 1992).

NOTES

LISTING OF CICERONE GUIDES

Via Ferratas of the French Alps
Walking in Corsica
Walking in Provence – East
Walking in Provence – West
Walking in the Auvergne
Walking in the Cevennes
Walking in the Dordogne
Walking in the Haute Savoie – North & South
Walking in the Tarentaise and Beaufortain Alps
Walks in the Cathar Region

GERMANY

Germany's Romantic Road
Hiking and Biking in the Black Forest
Walking in the Bavarian Alps

HIMALAYA

Annapurna
Bhutan
Everest
Garhwal and Kumaon
Langtang with Gosainkund and Helambu
Manaslu
The Mount Kailash Trek
Trekking in Ladakh
Trekking in the Himalaya

ICELAND & GREENLAND

Trekking in Greenland
Walking and Trekking in Iceland

IRELAND

The Irish Coast to Coast Walk
The Mountains of Ireland

ITALY

Gran Paradiso
Sibillini National Park
Shorter Walks in the Dolomites
The Way of St Francis
Through the Italian Alps
Trekking in the Apennines
Trekking in the Dolomites
Via Ferratas of the Italian Dolomites: Vols 1 & 2
Walking in Abruzzo
Walking in Italy's Stelvio National Park
Walking in Sardinia
Walking in Sicily
Walking in the Central Italian Alps
Walking in the Dolomites

Walking in Tuscany
Walking in Umbria
Walking on the Amalfi Coast
Walking the Italian Lakes

MEDITERRANEAN

Jordan – Walks, Treks, Caves, Climbs and Canyons
The Ala Dag
The High Mountains of Crete
The Mountains of Greece
Treks and Climbs in Wadi Rum
Walking and Trekking on Corfu
Walking in Malta
Western Crete

NORTH AMERICA

British Columbia
The Grand Canyon
The John Muir Trail
The Pacific Crest Trail

SOUTH AMERICA

Aconcagua and the Southern Andes
Hiking and Biking Peru's Inca Trails
Torres del Paine

SCANDINAVIA

Walking in Norway

SLOVENIA, CROATIA AND MONTENEGRO

The Islands of Croatia
The Julian Alps of Slovenia
The Mountains of Montenegro
Trekking in Slovenia
Walking in Croatia
Walking in Slovenia: The Karavanke

SPAIN AND PORTUGAL

Mountain Walking in Southern Catalunya
Spain's Sendero Histórico: The GR1
The Mountains of Nerja
The Northern Caminos
Trekking through Mallorca
Walking in Madeira
Walking in Mallorca
Walking in Menorca
Walking in the Algarve
Walking in the Cordillera Cantabrica
Walking in the Sierra Nevada

Walking on Gran Canaria
Walking on La Gomera and El Hierro
Walking on La Palma
Walking on Lanzarote and Fuerteventura
Walking on Tenerife
Walking the GR7 in Andalucia
Walks and Climbs in the Picos de Europa

SWITZERLAND

Alpine Pass Route
Central Switzerland
The Swiss Alps
Tour of the Jungfrau Region
Walking in the Bernese Oberland
Walking in the Valais
Walking in Ticino
Walks in the Engadine

TECHNIQUES

Geocaching in the UK
Indoor Climbing
Lightweight Camping
Map and Compass
Mountain Weather
Outdoor Photography
Polar Exploration
Rock Climbing
Sport Climbing
The Hillwalker's Manual

MINI GUIDES

Alpine Flowers
Avalanche!
Navigating with a GPS
Navigation
Pocket First Aid and Wilderness Medicine
Snow

MOUNTAIN LITERATURE

8000 metres
A Walk in the Clouds
Abode of the Gods
Unjustifiable Risk?

For full information on all our guides, books and eBooks, visit our website:
www.cicerone.co.uk.

Walking – Trekking – Mountaineering – Climbing – Cycling

Over 40 years, Cicerone have built up an outstanding collection of over 300 guides, inspiring all sorts of amazing adventures.

Every guide comes from extensive exploration and research by our expert authors, all with a passion for their subjects. They are frequently praised, endorsed and used by clubs, instructors and outdoor organisations.

All our titles can now be bought as **e-books**, **ePubs** and **Kindle** files and we also have an online magazine – **Cicerone Extra** – with features to help cyclists, climbers, walkers and trekkers choose their next adventure, at home or abroad.

Our website shows any **new information** we've had in since a book was published. Please do let us know if you find anything has changed, so that we can publish the latest details. On our **website** you'll also find great ideas and lots of detailed information about what's inside every guide and you can buy **individual routes** from many of them online.

It's easy to keep in touch with what's going on at Cicerone by getting our monthly **free e-newsletter**, which is full of offers, competitions, up-to-date information and topical articles. You can subscribe on our home page and also follow us on **Facebook** and **Twitter** or dip into our **blog**.

Cicerone – the very best guides for exploring the world.

CICERONE

2 Police Square Milnthorpe Cumbria LA7 7PY
Tel: 015395 62069 info@cicerone.co.uk
www.cicerone.co.uk and **www.cicerone-extra.com**